Joyful Manifestation

Ten Steps to Empower Yourself and
Attract a Happy and Successful Life

Sugandhi Iyer

BALBOA.
PRESS

A DIVISION OF HAY HOUSE

Balboa Press books may be ordered through booksellers or by contacting:

Balboa Press
A Division of Hay House
1663 Liberty Drive
Bloomington, IN 47403
www.balboapress.com
1 (877) 407-4847

Because of the dynamic nature of the Internet, any web addresses or links contained in this book may have changed since publication and may no longer be valid. The views expressed in this work are solely those of the author and do not necessarily reflect the views of the publisher, and the publisher hereby disclaims any responsibility for them.

The author of this book does not dispense medical advice or prescribe the use of any technique as a form of treatment for physical, emotional, or medical problems without the advice of a physician, either directly or indirectly. The intent of the author is only to offer information of a general nature to help you in your quest for emotional and spiritual well-being. In the event you use any of the information in this book for yourself, which is your constitutional right, the author and the publisher assume no responsibility for your actions.

Any people depicted in stock imagery provided by Thinkstock are models, and such images are being used for illustrative purposes only.
Certain stock imagery © Thinkstock.

Print information available on the last page.

ISBN: 978-1-4525-4046-7 (sc)
ISBN: 978-1-4525-4045-0 (e)

Balboa Press rev. date: 09/08/2015

Contents

PART III
The Process

PART IV
The Land of Joy and Miracles

Dedications

To my parents and the rest of my loving family.

To you, my readers and friends.

Let us intend to live joyfully; spreading love, joy, and abundance around this amazing world, for it belongs to us.

Love

Sugandhi Iyer

Preface

The idea for *Joyful Manifestation* formed over a few years. The first thought of writing a spiritually oriented success book came as I was going through a personal life event which made me seek answers to some of life's most complex questions. The answers I found are shared in this book with you. This book will help you understand who you really are, what you are here for, what you really want, and show you how to get it. It will show you how to succeed in life and to be happy while seeking the things you most desire.

The laws that govern me also govern you, and the knowledge that helped me will also help you. The law of gravity applies to us all; nobody is spared from it. In the same way, the laws of the universe apply to all those who are a part of this universe, as everyone is subject to the same universal forces. The trick lies in learning how to work with these forces using the knowledge given to you by various sources, to navigate life successfully.

Joyful Manifestation is a mix of spirituality and success. There are various flavors that you will encounter on your journey through this book as it does represent life. You may find it intense in places, sometimes light, and sometimes invigorating and dynamic. I will explain certain terminologies and principles to help you understand your life, and to work with the universe to get what you want.

There are affirmations in this book to help you get into alignment with your goals. You will find these affirmations in bold letters, italics, and within quotes. Other statements that I want to bring to your attention are in bold letters and italics, but without quotes. Instead of saying 'he/she' every time, I will use 'he' even though in most cases I am not being gender specific. I will also use 'he' for God, but as you know God includes both male and female, is in fact beyond gender, and is nothing and everything at the same time.

You will find me using the words God, Self, Source, Higher Self, Inner Self, Core Self, True Self, the All, the soul, the universe, and the Divine interchangeably sometimes, as they all refer to the same power of creation, known by different names. A brief explanation of some of these terms:

+ The Self, also known as the All, the Whole, Source, God, or Brahman, contains everything, including the personality that is you. Pure, because it is untouched by events, it includes the universe, the gods, and everything else, both dark and light. Though it includes the light and dark forces, the truth is that it is beyond the play of these forces.

+ The Higher Self, Inner Self, Core Self, and True Self are ways of referring to that part of the Self which is divine, joyous, and all knowing. It is the voice of knowledge that comes to the rescue, interested in your well-being and is the true part of you unaffected by the play of this world.

+ The soul is that part of the Self that can either limit itself to being a small part of the Whole, or expand into the Whole. The truth is that it is the Self itself.

+ The word *universe* is used in two ways. It includes your actual manifested world and the manifesting force(s). The manifesting forces act according to your inner world. Simply put, your outside world is created from your inner universe.

+ The Divine is the light aspect of the All. Being divine means embodying the light qualities at its best (it is a state that is free of darkness). It is the state of the Higher Self.

Ultimately, it is all you, the Self that wants to experience life.

Take your time with *Joyful Manifestation* because as you read this book you may have some consciousness shifts and 'aha' moments. Let the 'aha' moments happen as they change your energy and your vibrations. Take a deep breath and let the words in. Just allow. It's also okay if you are not ready for the changes. Just put the book aside and come back to the words later. Take your time and make only such self-changes that you feel comfortable with. There is no rush to master anything. In fact, use the word 'master' with care as it is only there to help you conquer anything that may come between you and your creations. Anytime you feel like judging yourself, let the feeling go and reconnect to your inner power and joy. The true nature of your Self is joy, and when you find joy you find everything, because the vibration of joy is the highest of the creation vibrations in this world and is like your magic wand. Remember, joy is your true nature and the only one worth keeping. Happy reading!

Love,

Sugandhi Iyer

PART I

Manifestation is Joyful

"It has been and always will be my joy that creates joyful situations. No other ingredient is required, except maybe a dollop of self-empowerment."

Chapter One

Introduction to Joyful Manifestation

*"You are the Source of it all, and
this Source is joy itself."*

W ithin you is a storehouse of something that lies low, just waiting to be experienced. It can be described in one word, 'Source,' as it is the source from which everything flows, including the knowledge that fuels creation.

This universe is created on the foundation of knowledge which pervades everything and is everywhere. When connected to Source, you have access to this knowledge. Many have connected to this knowledge in the past, and many still do, because every problem can be solved and every need fulfilled just by tapping into it.

Depending on their interests, people receive the information they require. If one is a scientist, one receives ideas and breakthroughs; if a spiritualist, one receives knowledge of the Spirit; and if an explorer, one receives knowledge about the world and its places. Since Source is also pure power, amazing feats and tasks can be handled when connected to this power, and you can create like Source would. Since Source is joy, peace, power, and love, all of your manifestations have no choice but to be joyful when they come from Source.

When you realize that you are Source, how much more powerful your manifestations will be!

What does Joyful Manifestation have to do with this?

Manifestation is the transformation of spirit into physical form. Your material world is a reflection of your inner world and when your inner world contains excitement, delight, power, and joy, whatever you do happens from this space and brings back manifestations that embody that happiness, giving you cause for celebration. As you introduce joy into your inner psychological world, you will see your material world change and reflect that joy back to you.

As you change your focus, what you focus on also changes. While 'abundance consciousness' manifests as abundance in your life, 'lack consciousness' manifests as physical lack in your world. This lack manifests again and again until you make a conscious change. Since suffering or sadness gets physically manifested as lack, all manifestation—both conscious and unconscious—should come from the space of love, joy, and confidence. As you become more conscious of abundance, you will learn to be situated in joy more often, and this joy in turn manifests more abundance. It's like depositing a sum of money in a CD and watching it grow while collecting interest, or like planting seeds and eating the fruits born by the trees that come out of those seeds. The fruits that you get depend on some factors like:

1. The seeds you plant,

2. The water and sunlight the plant/tree receives,

3. The health of the ground,

4. Your patience and care.

Once you plant the seeds of your life in joy, they will grow into joyful events. Even if undesired situations happen, you can use the Joyful Manifestation process to get back into a successful space. When you hit the vibration of joy with respect to any life area, it returns joy back to you.

> *Your single-minded determination to allow joy to be your guiding star is what gets you to where you want to go.*

The vibration of joy is so powerful that lower vibrations cannot win or even survive in its light. When you become a Joyful Manifester you will live in a space of joy and your mind will feel good about itself and life in general. When you feel good, you become well-situated to attract good to yourself. Even if you were physically lost somewhere, if you could just connect to your joy, you would manifest being found.

When joy and abundance become your points of focus, you will have the Law of Attraction working to your advantage. You may have had moments and phases when you've had an easy flow of events, but in those life areas where you keep encountering hurdles, you can use the Joyful Manifestation process to get what you want to flow easily into your life.

Joyful Manifestation happens when you start becoming one with who you really are. When you realize that you are Source and connect to this truth, you become joyful, and manifest joyful situations. As you understand who you are, what your purpose is, and how this universe works, you will be better situated to walk toward the reality that you *really* want to see happen, rather than just being compelled to deal with situations.

> *Your life journey is all about getting into the space of true joy and creating what you want from that space. You should know that you attract good situations easily, because it is natural for you to do so. Go ahead and Joyfully Manifest your life.*

Chapter Two

~

Manifestation

*"I am here to manifest my life experiences
in a way that gives me joy."*

Why is the word *manifestation* so important these days? When I was growing up, I had not heard this word being used as it is nowadays. More people are talking about manifesting their life events now, than before.

*It's almost as if the power of the gods has
been brought down to the people.*

So what is manifestation?

Manifestation is the process of creation. Basically, everything is in a state of unmanifest before it takes form and manifests. Before actual physical manifestation, everything is space, and in this space when thoughts occur, spirit moves energy to start a process of happening into physical form. After some time, when a physical form is no longer required, it is manifested

4

back into space (demanifestation). There is always a process happening; from the unmanifest into manifest, and then back into the unmanifest. The Self (Source) is always kept intact during this process, because it is pure consciousness. It is just the physical forms that come into and out of existence as and when the Self desires. For example, if the Self has a vision of a garden filled with beautiful roses, this idea remains in space until energy forms into a garden of roses which is the actual physical manifestation of the vision. When this garden is no longer required, it is unmanifested or transformed by another idea.

The mind is an extension of the light of the Core Self, and contains the programming relevant to the personality (that which makes one tick) and pervades and forms the body. Some of the programming is well known, as it is in the conscious mind, while some of it is still unknown, as it is contained in the subconscious mind.

You become aware of this hidden programming when you come across certain situations that you finally understand to be patterns arising from the working of your mind and its tendencies, and your vibrational attraction factor. If something is happening, just know that it is happening because your mind contains instructions that attract people, situations, and things to you, causing you to act and react in certain ways. It is essential to change this programming in order for you to change your manifestations.

Manifestation is much more practical than what it is sometimes portrayed to be, and it is very much in your power to change your manifestations by changing your attraction of situations.

Manifestation happens all the time with or without you knowing it. You are always manifesting your life situations, and these manifestations happen according to the space that your mind is in.

Manifestation of desires

Manifestation of desires is important because born into this material world, the importance of creation cannot be ignored. There are various schools of thought that totally discount the importance of the desires that fuel creation, and label them as bad or sinful. You are in a physical world, and it is imperative to respect the intentions of the creation force behind this world which uses desire as a tool of inspiration for creation. The skill lies in understanding these desires and working with them consciously to understand your life purpose, and the setting and implementation of useful and happy life goals.

Discovering who you are is important

The healthy and happy manifestation of life events rests entirely on the healthy and happy state of your mind which, when situated in positive thoughts, creates positive outcomes. To this end, discovering yourself and being aware of who you really are is important, otherwise your mind gets overcome by negative experiences, feels defeated, and gives into sadness and depression, creating a hotbed for even more negativity. Your mind is used to seeing only the external world as the truth and is unaware of its real truth, being untrained to look within and recognize its true identity. Since it is unaware of its true identity, it gets confused and stressed. Your mind has to register its real truth and purpose, bringing you into alignment with what you want. When your mind feels better about itself, it will be able to retain a confident and positive outlook on life.

There is more on the subject of who you really are in Part II of this book, but the following information will help for now.

You are a 'being' experiencing life, and for all purposes you can consider this 'being' as playing three separate roles, each role played in order to get the most intensive and expansive life experience. You can also understand it in this way; you are made up of three parts:

1. A core spark (your higher aspect) which retains its original carefree, joyful nature, is completely untouched by life events, and has a wide perspective of it *all*.

2. Your personality, created by your birth and life situations and subject to change and influences, which is the focused physical aspect of your being into this world.

3. The world that you deal with everyday, with which your personality interacts to have its life experience.

Yes, you are the Higher Self, the physical manifested being, and the universe, each one working with the others to get the best life experience possible. The need to understand that you are it all is important, because it stops the feeling of the world as being separate from you. It is not separate. It is you, or a part of you, as you are much more than just the focused physical person having a singular, pointed experience.

RESIDE IN THE SPACE OF JOY

The issue, if any, is that while the core of you knows that it is joy itself, your personality often loses track of this truth because of its constant involvement with the external world and its drama. You, the physical being, are unaware of the truth of who you really are. Under the constant push and pull of this external world, you often don't identify with the real you, which is joy. Your Self is joy and if you are able to connect to your joy, you can bring this joy into your world and see it reflected everywhere. Free of the negatives of life, you would experience great health, happiness, wealth, and all that a joyful mind could conceptualize.

A joyful mind is one that is located in its true and joyful nature, free of the play of negativity, and it is in this space of being located in joy and having positive feelings and expectations that joyful events are manifested. Since the normal tendency is to have thoughts and perform actions according to the mental space you are in, it is best to watch this space and keep shifting it into happiness.

The space you are in creates your life. This is the simplest way to sum up the art of manifestation.

Since all physical space is the result of your mental space, it is best to keep this mental space in joy.

Think of a room in your house. How is this room? Is it comfortable, crowded, roomy, beautiful, well-lit, happy, or gloomy? This room reflects your taste in décor and your affordability. It reflects you and the space you are currently in. Of course, you could be completely detached from your room and what it looks like, but still the very fact of your detachment is reflected in your taste. If you were a monk, it could be that the room is decorated very simply, and you may even sleep on the floor. Then the other extreme; think of the opulent harems maintained by some kings for their pleasure—and you know what I am speaking off. The activities of the harems reflect their mood and décor. Whatever you do while in this room reflects the mood of the room and what it means to you. Your energy is intertwined with the mood of the room and it with yours, and all manifestation happens accordingly. The physical space you are in reflects you, and whatever you manifest in it reflects that physical space.

Let's say that you actually have luxurious tastes, but because of affordability issues are not able to decorate your room in the manner that you would like. The fact of your non-affordability is reflected in your home. Don't feel bad now; there is a god or goddess within you who knows that you can afford anything and it is this god or goddess that we aim to bring out. So even while observing your current situation, stop feeling bad about it, and let it go. As you understand who you are and consciously change your space, the way that life treats you changes for the better, and the Law of Attraction has no choice but to bring you evidence of that wonderful change. Manifestation is easy for those who rest in their happy Self.

Chapter Three

~

The Law of Attraction

"As I feel happy and abundant, more happiness and abundance finds me. The Law of Attraction is always working to my advantage."

T hings that fit together will always come together to create a whole. It is the natural tendency of the universe to bring its creations together. It brings together man and woman, child and parents, the thirsty and water, and the hungry and food. This universe is always supplying to its creations, satisfying hunger, quenching thirst, and fulfilling demands. This is the natural order of things. Desires arise from all of God's creations, and the universe rushes to fulfill them.

The parent aspect of the universe ensures that all of God's creations are taken care of. The more evolved the creations, the more complex are its wants and desires. The universe addresses this complexity of desires by enabling man to discover, invent, and suitably meet situations. This process of bringing together demand and supply is in place to nurture creation.

After all, these are the Divine's creations, and what the Divine creates must be maintained, right?

Now here are some of the million dollar questions that people ask: If the universe is always fulfilling desires, why then does lack exist? Why does it seem as if desires are not being fulfilled? Why are people left with a sinking hole in their hearts after witnessing one disheartening situation after another? Why do ill health, scarcity, want, violence, and impoverishment gain such footholds in people's minds? Why is there so much disparity in this world? Why is it that war wages within the same universe, the same world, the same nation, and in the same person?

The reason for all of these seeming abnormalities is the intentional play of light and dark energies in various combinations introduced into creation to enable full life experiences. The duality, with its many varying shades in between, creates a fascinating playground where life is experienced in its fullness. The dualities of supply and demand, light and dark, good and bad are worked through the operation of certain universal laws, one of which is the Law of Attraction.

Since the universe constantly seeks to create a whole by supplying to its creations' demands, as soon as a person experiences some hunger, the universe swoops in to satisfy this desire. However, even while the desire for food is experienced and the food is supplied to the hungry person, there are two self-defeating and counterproductive actions that a person can take:

1. Either he pounces on the food and gobbles it down quickly from fear that he will not get food again, which means that he continues to hold onto the lack energy, or

2. He may not allow food in and continues to experience hunger. For example, he may be so hungry, fearful, and angry that he may block sources of that food from reaching him.

The two extreme reactions are responsible for most people's discontentment, which adds to their feeling of lack, which keeps them in the old energies of hunger, not moving into a new energy of fulfillment.

What influence a person's responses are his beliefs. A belief is a thought that has remained with a person for a very long time, cementing itself into his consciousness as a truth. This belief, instead of being helpful to the person, actually acts as a hindrance to good coming in. This is called resistance and is the result of the nature of thoughts that a person has. Since every thought has a vibration, thoughts with the most energy create a dominant vibration that attracts situations that match the vibration, just like setting the radio dial to 101.3 brings you whatever is being broadcast on 101.3. Abundance or lack is perpetuated because of the nature of thoughts that a person has and their dominant vibration.

> ### The Law of Attraction works on the basis that like attracts like and so your dominant thoughts will attract like situations.

To 'attract' means to draw to oneself; to exert a force on something causing it to approach or prevent it from moving away. A beautiful woman by virtue of the knowledge of her beauty attracts the admiring stares of many. A knowledgeable and talented person by virtue of the awareness of his knowledge or talent draws to himself the respect of others. The keyword is 'awareness.' As you become aware of your goodness, or that of the world, the awareness vibrates in your energy and attracts many beneficial situations. The contrast is where negative impressions draw in negative situations that constantly reinforce the negativity.

Once you have a thought, your mind either gives the thought attention or lets it go. What motivates your mind to give a thought attention is if that thought has a charge, either a positive or negative one. A positive charge means that the mind likes the thought and finds pleasure in it and a negative charge means that your mind does not like the thought and what it means to its peaceful existence.

Once the mind decides that it wants to pursue a thought (and many times it is forced to do so because of what we call fatal attraction) it starts to mull on it, and soon many thoughts of like nature are called. The mind now finds itself dealing with many thoughts of the same vibration, which then creates a mood. Once a mood starts to set in, it motivates actions. Your vibrations are also set for something to happen since these like thoughts create a dominant point of attraction, which pulls to you like situations that seem to reinforce the original thought. Thus, things keep on happening to you, and you either enjoy or suffer the happenings.

LIGHT BEINGS

Every person, and in fact every part of creation, is light and is constantly emanating light, the extent of light determining the vibration; the more light, the higher the vibration.

Speaking in terms of people, the higher the vibration of being, the higher is the frequency of the situations attracted back to the person. Each life area carries its own vibration which is contained in a person's energy, and depending on the vibration of a particular life area, matching situations are attracted. Worry is dark, and happiness is light with varying shades of gray in between. The more worry contained your energy with regard to a life area, the more worrisome are the situations attracted back.

The Law of Attraction is always working; tick-tock-tick-tock, it does its job. Like the law of gravity, it applies to everyone living in this time-space continuum, and was put into place by the Creating Mind in order to be able to play the game of life. You and your people are the players; life is the play board; thought and action are the dice, and life's situations and consequences are squares on the board that you reach due to the numbers displayed on the dice. In this game of life, you are the only player who can make a difference in your life, and the most powerful tool you have is your mind.

In this world of energy, there is a magnetic process of attraction and repelling happening all the time. The attraction forces bring things together, and the repelling forces keep things apart. What contribute to attraction forces are desire, knowledge, liking, maturity, open mindedness, and confidence. What contribute to repelling forces are ignorance, immaturity, doubt, dislike, and false perceptions.

YOUR POINT OF ATTRACTION

At any time you are giving out a signal that is a point of attraction calling forth experiences. This point of attraction is that point of your vibrations which is most accentuated at any time.

A thought, which is the result of your consciousness, is a unit of energy and has power. The extent of its power determines its creation potential, and the type of power it has determines whether it will attract positive or negative situations. The higher the vibration of the thought in terms of purity, self-confidence, love, and joy, the greater is its capacity to attract positive, high vibration situations. A thought may or may not be known to you and may exist more as a belief rather than something that you are consciously processing. In fact, when something does come into your conscious mind as a thought, it gives you a chance to observe and change it unless it has so much power that it sways your actions. Even after this happens and your actions produce a result that you experience and don't like, you still retain the power of changing the belief that originated the thought and resulting experience(s).

A powerful thought overrules other thoughts of weaker nature to create an attraction point for you, and the nature of the thought determines the nature of your attraction point and your responses. For example, if you have a thought that is loving toward someone, but another thought exists of anger or indifference, and this thought is more powerful as it has been in existence for a longer time, the negative thought being more powerful will attract negative situations to you and you will respond according to the emotions brought about by that powerful negative thought. If, however, you deliberately use your free will to think of more loving thoughts, release the negative, and thereby feed the love energy, your attraction point and your resulting responses change. You will be in the position to act lovingly and change your life.

The power to change your beliefs always lies with you, enabling you to change your point of attraction and change other's beliefs about you.

Your vibrations contain many elements to them, some of which are strong and some weak, created by your beliefs. The vibrations are of varying strengths and are about many life areas and topics. A huge part of your vibrations are carried forth from childhood and past lives, which have formed imprints in your soul energy. In each life, the soul balances its energy, keeping what it wants and getting rid of what it finds redundant.

When the time comes for your soul to balance an aspect of its energy, it attracts provocations which bring up the imprint(s) that it wants to change. Out of the blue you may be faced with a situation (that you may or may not have initiated) which then gets you to start thinking. You are left with the unenviable job of managing the situation and neutralizing the point of attraction which comes up for changing. You are given the opportunity to rid yourself of an unwanted vibe and to change it to something that would benefit you. Hidden somewhere in the mire of your vibes, this particular vibe was probably not serving you, and when it is time for more good fortune to pour on you, your soul brings up the imprint which needs to be tackled for useful change to happen so that it (your soul) can continue to expand its experiences. Even if no physical situation is used as a provocation, somewhere within you may arise the need to expand, and this starts a process of realization.

For example, an actress starring in small roles could start to wonder why she is getting urges to sign bigger budget movies, or to star in different roles of meaning, and she will get an urge to take action and expand. From within comes this feeling that something needs doing. It can also happen that she is taunted for being a small time actress, which then makes her decide to make it big (external physical situations causing a change). If this actress can train her personality to expand and become that amazing actress, she will have done most of the job, and as her mind expands and strengthens, she will naturally walk into big budget, star roles.

Each vibration that you change into a better one changes your attraction factor for the better.

Simply being aware that the Law of Attraction exists is not the key; it is only a first step. The key lies in consciously changing yourself and making it easy for the Law of Attraction to bring you good. Changing yourself means changing your inner world, which is governed by your beliefs and results in thoughts and actions. You do this by making useful mental shifts. It does not mean becoming a good person from the space of being bad; it just means becoming more of what you want to see happen. As your awareness changes, it reflects in your vibrations, attracting better situations.

So if you think that you are not beautiful, think otherwise. Think that you are beautiful and your being is that of beauty, and you will attract like situations proving you right. The element of changing yourself happens from the space of seeing what is constructive and destructive for you. Instead of vibrating 'victim,' become someone who is situated in peaceful self-empowerment. If you vibrate 'non-committal,' become capable of commitment instead. The best way to become committed to life is to change patterns and habits that will establish your being in commitment.

From the inner to the outer does it flow.

As you change your inner world, your consciousness changes, creating a new point of attraction, which then calls forth the energy of new experiences.

Controlling external situations helps, but only to the extent that you can successfully make changes in them. Sooner or later there will be those situations that you find you cannot change by dealing with them externally. When you have those moments when you know that inspite of all the sweetness, pushing, prodding, and arguing you just cannot change a situation, you are left with only one choice; become quiet, go back to yourself, and resolve whatever inside of you is creating the situations. Inner change before you take action is the best way, as it will bring back happy experiences. Even if you did take action from an old space of negativity, once you understand what's happening, your subsequent actions can be different, attracting different results.

If you continue to believe, think, and act the way you always have, the formulas and equations you have set in place continue to operate in the same way, churning out the same results again and again, with the Law of Attraction bringing you situations that keep reaffirming your beliefs.

As you become more skilled at dealing with your mind and your inner world, your external world becomes a wonderful reflection of this happier inner world, and each external action flows beautifully from this elevated space of being a Master Manifester. Become a magnet to attract abundance now.

Chapter Four

Abundance

"This world is abundant, and I am always taken care of. Wherever I look, there is an abundance of what I like and prefer."

So what is abundance?

Abundance means 'plenty of' and within the context of manifestation, refers to what you consider to be positive in life. Simply put, abundance is the state of profusion and wonderful fullness.

This universe is a place of abundance and if something does not already exist, the universe gives mankind abundant resources in the form of ideas and materials to create it with. You will find abundance everywhere; in the spread of flowers, stars, sunshine, and rain. As you become aware of the abundance that already exists in this universe, you start to feel the presence of abundance in your own life, and feeling abundance creates actual physical abundance.

AND THE OPPOSITE STATE ... LACK ...

Even though abundance is evident everywhere, because of this world of dualities, people can sometimes experience lack in their lives. Lack is present for quite a few people around the world, and if there is any disease in the world, it is lack.

Lack is the 'feeling' that you have been denied something that you want, that others seem to attract very easily, whether or not, in your opinion, they deserve it. Constantly feeling lack gives rise to actual physical lack, ending up in insecurity, sadness, depression and even disease.

Lack can easily be triggered by an event. For example, take the instance of Tom who found that the first woman he really liked turned him down. The rejection triggers something that was lying dormant in his subconscious mind, resulting in a series of rejections. This example can be applied to any life area.

All that lack needs is a small trigger and what starts out as a small spark could end up becoming a large forest fire. Feeling lack creates actual physical lack and it is best to reduce its importance from it being a truth to being just a thought to be easily dismissed at will.

While lack requires a very small trigger to establish itself in a person's life, abundance on the other hand, may require a lot of evidence before a person can start to think of himself as fortunate. People require a million or trillion dollars in their bank accounts before it registers on all levels of their consciousness that they are financially well off and sound. A lot of people need thousands of people telling them that they are beautiful before they can believe that they are truly beautiful. However, it takes only one small, mean comment to get someone to start considering himself as unattractive.

So basically, while lack needs very little fuel to get established in your mind, abundance may have to knock on your door several thousand times a day before you start to consider your universe as abundant. Why not make the universe's job easier and start to feel abundance now?

An affirmation:

"I love this world abundantly, and this world returns this love back to me abundantly. There is an abundance of wealth and resources available to me to create my life with, and I use these resources with complete love and respect."

Desires

The feeling of abundance or lack depends upon the fulfillment or non-fulfillment of your desires. When your desires get fulfilled consistently, it creates feelings of abundance, and when your desires remain unfulfilled for some time, it creates feelings of lack. These feelings then contribute by drawing in more lack or abundance. What came first, the egg or the chicken? Does it matter if the physical lack gave rise to the feelings of lack, or the feelings of lack gave rise to physical lack? It does not matter at all. What matters is that you can do something about it. When you feel happy that your natural desires are fulfilled easily, you start to feel the presence of abundance, instead of lack, in your life.

Since desires are what fuel the states of abundance and lack, let's take a look at this very interesting topic upon which the whole of creation revolves. The Law of Attraction teachings recommend moving confidently toward your desires without fear of non-achievement, and while the best case scenario is to move confidently toward the fulfillment of your desires without the fear of loss, it may not always be possible. It is wise to know a few things about the subject of desire so that you can know how to work with your genuine desires to allow them to attain fulfillment, and save you the stress that results from the constant push and pull that happens in difficult situations.

Proper information helps you deal with life successfully.

Chapter Five

~

Desires—Can't Live With Them, Can't Live Without Them!

"My desires are fueled by enthusiasm and allow me to experience expansion. They are well balanced, healthy, and completely in alignment with who I am and who I am becoming."

The ancient Indian text *Srimad Bhagwatam* (which means that which is spoken by God) contains a narrative which says that when the Creator God 'Brahma' (derived from the word *Brahman*, which is the All) first created mankind, he created only enlightened beings like sages who were not interested in material perpetuation and other procreation activities, and immediately went into states of deep trance. They were not interested in life and were only interested in experiencing the Divine in states of deep contemplation and meditation. Soon, the Creator God Brahma realized his mistake, and created people with desires for materialistic and procreation activities and life started happening.

This whole creation is based on desires. Desires result in the expansion of the universe as life perpetuates. Without the desires that fuel creation, life itself would cease to exist. All that is required are a lot of uninterested people who think that life is useless, and that's it; life as you know it would stop.

A desire can best be described as an urge that arises from within you to do something, to possess something, or to be something, the thought of accomplishing which gives rise to a feeling of happiness and fulfillment. The feeling of happiness associated with the fulfillment of the desire is usually proportionate to the importance that you give to the person, thing, or situation for which you have the desire. Different people allocate different positions of importance to different things. Not all people give the same level of importance to all life areas, and as each person cultivates his or her own likes and dislikes, desires arise accordingly. For example, businessmen have the desire to grow their business and spend a lot of time in business related activities.

This world needs entrepreneurs, scientists, doctors, teachers, athletes, singers, actors, cleaners, etc. Since this world needs to be maintained, your purpose will rise up in you as a desire or an enthusiasm to do something and depending upon the importance that it holds for you, you may be compelled to take suitable action to fulfill your desires as they arise. All you have to do is to get ready, allow it to happen, and then receive.

A person who knows how to work with the laws of manifestation is aware that it is not the desire that will make or break his enthusiasm, but that it is his enthusiasm that will make or break a desire.

When enthusiasm for a certain life area or a person or thing wanes, it means that this desire is reducing. It is enthusiasm that fuels a desire, taking it into successful manifestation. Despondent feelings do not result in Joyful

Manifestation. In the space of Joyful Manifestation, a desire is more of an enthusiasm which, when it rises up (and sometimes even before it rises up) and becomes known to the person, is fulfilled. Natural enthusiasm takes you smoothly to natural and wonderful conclusions. A desire that lacks enthusiasm will get you to lose energy quickly, and deflates chances of positive manifestation. If you don't work on the negative energy of the desire itself, it becomes karmic (explained in the next section) losing its purity and natural ability of self-fulfillment.

PURE DESIRES VS. KARMIC DESIRES

Karma means action and includes inaction. However, the common usage of this word indicates the consequences attached to each action or inaction (there is more on this fascinating subject in chapter 16). Karmic energy could be good or bad, but in the context of differentiating between a pure desire and a karmic one, I am using the term 'karmic' to indicate accumulation of a negative charge to a life area. It is when a life area becomes karmic that difficulty in its natural fulfillment arises.

A *pure desire* gets fulfilled automatically with no stress, has no negative energy of defeat attached to it, and no questions about its fulfillment. It gets fulfilled all by itself with very little and stress-free action required from you. It's like having a desire for a burger and buying that burger, or two people meeting, falling in love and getting married, or someone making an offer to sell a home and getting a suitable buyer quickly. Your body goes through the actions automatically, almost as if no thought were required in the process of fulfillment. Your self-worth does not get called into question in the case of pure desires. Pure desires are easy to fulfill simply because of the level of your confidence in knowing that it is possible, and as you feel empowered for it to happen, it happens by itself, very naturally.

A desire which has tones of impossibility, sadness, and difficulty attached to it is *karmic* in nature, and gives rise to further issues that bind. It creates stress in the mind, doubt in your self-worth, and many times doubt in creation itself. Sometimes fulfilling a karmic desire becomes so difficult that you end up wanting freedom from that desire itself.

When exposed to a karmic desire, emotions run riot, hurt becomes your playground, and sometimes all hell can break loose. Your negative point of attraction is at a high in karmic situations, and the actions taken in karmic modes are negative, adding more hurt to the situation. It is this type of desire that most people seek freedom from and start seeking peace of mind. After being exposed to karmic desires, people usually start having a greater desire for freedom. For example, a woman may want a particular man to fall in love with her. Her desire starts seeking fulfillment and she may take action toward its fulfillment. Some way through this experience however, she finds that her quest for love is taking more effort than is required, and her feelings keep getting hurt. Even though she would love to have the man fall in love with her, she finds that she has a greater desire to be free of the situation and starts working at falling out of love.

Such situations are common and happen everywhere in some form or the other. People want something, find that they are having a difficult time getting it, and then start praying for freedom of mind and from the situation itself, because of a feeling of lack of control.

So how does one handle such situations? Should you kill your desire and lose all hope? Or should you continue to try?

When faced with a karmic desire ask yourself the following questions:

1. Is what I desire really healthy for me in the long run?

2. Will it be a source of continued joy to me?

3. Is it only my ego that requires an acknowledgement of its self-worth through the continued pursuit of this desire?

4. How much emotion am I putting behind this desire, and what is the nature of the emotion; sadness, anger, joy?

5. Is there a sense of purpose to this? Does this help in my growth?

6. Will my desire be fulfilled by something else? Is there something better waiting for me?

7. Am I able to retain my sense of enthusiasm, or is it becoming harder and harder for me to do so?

8. Can I regain my sense of enthusiasm with some good thoughts?

Keep the following words in mind:

> ***"My desire is fueled by my enthusiasm. Without enthusiasm, desire is a just like a dried up well."***

Always bring back the enthusiasm into a situation because your enthusiasm is the main ingredient for successful manifestation. For example, if you start a business and don't find profits rolling in, how do you feel? Are you ready to give up the business? If you feel that you are not ready to give it up, let go of the need to see profits for a while and focus instead on the feeling of enthusiasm you initially had for the business and the creation work involved. This enthusiasm for the business with or without profits will fuel the manifestation of profits. As long as you feel enthusiastic, you are doing well. Work with your thoughts, beliefs, and emotions to enthusiastically and joyfully manifest your life.

Chapter Six

∼

Your Thoughts
and Beliefs

*"I have happy thoughts which arise
from beliefs that are healthy for me.
I am always manifesting good."*

A thought is an idea, an image, or a concept that is born out of your consciousness. Your mind constantly churns out thoughts at a very high rate. Some of them capture your fascination, while others die away by themselves as you ignore them.

Thoughts happen either because an old image comes to mind, or a new one comes up from within you. There is a thinker, and contrary to what you imagine, the thinker is not you, the physical person. It is your Inner Self, the core of you that wants to experience life, which is why you may sometimes be stunned with some of the ideas that you get because they just 'come up' from within you and you go, "Aha!" Good thoughts that come up from within need to be paid attention to as they could be inspirations. Thoughts that happen because of past images coming alive in the mind may or may not be paid attention to. That's your choice and is based entirely on whether or not you want to give them power.

A belief is a concept that gives rise to thoughts of the same nature. The concept was created from thoughts that stayed around for some time, and you ended up believing them by seeing them proven true again and again. It could also be something that the society that you move in holds as a belief, and so having been exposed to it, you make it your truth. When you believe something, your thoughts happen accordingly, and you then act (action includes inaction) upon it. A thought that you believe in has power and contributes to your vibrations. It does not matter whether it is positive or negative except to the extent of the consequences it attracts. It gains power from its sheer existence and your mere attention to it.

- As you believe you think, desire, and intend.

- What you think and believe, you vibrate.

- What you vibrate, you attract.

- What you attract, you react to.

- How you react creates consequences and outcomes.

- The consequences reinstate or negate your beliefs, and affect your enthusiasm.

- Your enthusiasm affects your desires, intentions and thoughts.

- What you think and believe, you vibrate.

A cycle is going on here, and if you are not happy with the outcomes you are witnessing, then take a step back and break the cycle of thoughts. For any event there is a chain of happenings, and if you can break even one link in the chain of belief, thought, and action, you could shift the outcome.

For example, Harold stayed up watching movies late into the night, eating pizza and drinking beer. The next day, he woke up with a headache and left for work later than usual. His boss was angry and gave him a lecture on tardiness. Harold is now upset because his ego is hurt. He drove home that evening in a bad mood, distracted from his normally careful driving habits. Mark was rushing to the airport to pick up his wife and was trying to make up time by driving fast. Harold and Mark collided at an intersection.

There is a chain of events which lead up to this accident. If either of the two people involved in the accident had broken even one link in the chain of events leading to the accident, it would not have happened.

If Harold had gone to bed on time and not stayed up late, he would not have been tired, which means that he would have woken up on time and made it to work. His day would have started on a good note, and unless something else happened to upset his day, Harold would have spent the day in a good mood, driven home safely, been alert to other rash drivers, and not have had an accident. Harold cannot control events outside of him (for example, he could not have prevented Mark from rushing), but he could control his own thoughts and actions. Suppose Harold has a belief system where he should not stay up late drinking. He would think "It's time to hit the sack" and would have gone to sleep on time. Another belief system resulting in correct thinking and action which could have helped break the chain is, "Well, even if my boss did yell at me, it's okay, because I was late. I'm glad that he pointed it out to me, as I have learned a valuable lesson here which will help me in my future, whether in this job or another." Harold would have put his boss's lecture behind him and spent the rest of the day without stress. This would mean that he would have been in a good mood while driving home and could have avoided the accident. Another practice that would have helped Harold is to notice when his mood was off, and not drive until he calmed himself enough to feel good again.

Your beliefs make all the difference to how you think, act, and behave.

For example, the belief that this book will do a wealth of good for the world had me thinking positive thoughts about it, which fueled the desire for its completion, and I took action. I sat down and wrote it, and the universe swooped in and got it published. What if I was besieged with thoughts of not being qualified enough or good enough, or was even lazy and unenthusiastic? The thoughts I would have had would have been against the successful completion of this book, and it would not be in your hands now.

Positive thoughts create enthusiasm, which fuels your desires, helps you take positive action, and have positive and happy results. Think positive thoughts.

Chapter Seven

Emotions

"My thoughts trigger emotions that are always in alignment with joy. I let go of those thoughts that create emotions that make me feel less than who I really am. I am joy and I focus on feeling good!"

EMOTIONS; WHAT A BLESSING, AND YET THEY CAN SOMETIMES BE A CURSE

What a blessing, because otherwise this dormant consciousness would not be able to experience life in all its magnificent colors; what a curse, because when fueled by intense emotions, life experiences can get out of hand. I am sure that every person reading these words has experienced deep emotions, sometimes even heavy and unbearably intense.

Emotions add color to life. The flutter of the heart while awaiting a loved one; the tears of gratitude that well up when receiving something precious; the affection that a mother feels while looking at the smiling faces of her children; the pride that a father feels when his young ones do well; the devotion that one feels for God; the elation that a CEO feels when his company meets its sales targets, are examples of the different types of positive emotions that one can experience in life.

The human nervous system, with its very delicate bio-chemical makeup, is a highly evolved mechanism designed to register physical and mental experiences and to respond to them suitably. Depending on the experience, a person can feel pleasant emotions like peace, love, happiness, and joy, or unpleasant ones like sadness, anger, hatred, and revenge. In fact, it is not even necessary to go through an experience personally, but just the thought of something traumatic or ecstatic can create sad or happy emotions and reactions.

> *The soul uses the human body with its nervous system to experience life, and to discover what it likes and does not like, creating its preferences and life experiences accordingly. The human body is the means by which the soul tastes life.*

THOUGHTS, BELIEFS AND EMOTIONS

The bundle of thoughts that you have, which arise from your beliefs about yourself and the world around you, form your very unique energy vibration, attracting situations to you. Each person is an energy bundle offering his vibrations to the universe, and what you experience is a result of that very unique vibration that you are offering. What you experience happens because of the collection of thoughts around you.

You may not have control over your past thoughts, but you do have the power to:

+ Observe your current line of thoughts, and

+ Shift to a new way of thinking and resultant enthusiasm, desires, intentions, vibrations, actions, and consequences.

It is very much within your power to work with your thoughts consciously, using your emotions as a highly advanced guidance system.

The thoughts you think trigger feelings in you. When you have a thought about something that you like or dislike, you experience pleasure or pain. If you catch hold of the thought and keep running it through your mind, you will have access to other matching thoughts, which then ends up creating a mood of either pleasure or pain. Other events, joys, fears, expectations having the same vibration will have access to your mind and lend credence to your beliefs. The mood gets stronger and stronger until you are forced to take some action. The nature of action you take will depend on:

- The type of mood you are in. If your thoughts made you happy, you may call up your buddy in joy and tell him that you love him. If your thoughts made you unhappy, depending on your nature you may cry, vent your feelings, retreat, etc.

- How much power such a mood has to shake you. The power of a mood to push you into action depends entirely on how many similar moods you have had in the past. There is always the last straw on the camel's back. Happy moods of course are cause for celebration, and so you may end up celebrating.

Repeated negative thoughts can create depression, and repeated negative emotions can create violence.

What should you do when besieged by negative thoughts that give rise to negative emotions?

Change your thoughts, and change your perspective immediately. Nothing is worth the negative emotions that you may experience as a result of negative thoughts, because each time you experience negativity, toxins are released into your body not to mention the physical actions that you may be forced to take as a result of the negativity. The worst emotions are experienced when backed up by past incidents that lend weight to the current one. The intensity of the emotions also depends on the importance of the subject matter in question. The type of emotions you feel depend entirely on what you hold important. The subjects of life, health, money, land, relationships, power, and reputation have very significant places in people's minds. History is full of wars that have been fought to gain or retain love, power, and possessions. The negative thoughts you hold onto are like garbage. Always work on ridding yourself of the mental garbage collected everyday so that trauma energy is not built into your system. Just like you dispose the garbage in your home and don't store it (as the nature of garbage is to decompose, stink and collect vermin), in the same way you should dispose the negative happenings of each day. Let your thoughts melt away into the ethers, and/or call on your angels and hand over your thoughts on a plate for purification. Let go of all negative attachments. Distract yourself with music, dance, or exercise.

The complete opposite to the feeling of trauma is the feeling of gratitude. When you feel gratitude, it is normally for things that matter to you. It is the feeling of thankfulness for what is already with you, or coming to you. When you feel gratitude, you know that your life is going well and that everything is just right with the universe.

Gratitude is the acknowledgement of God's presence in your life. The presence of God is grace. Grace keeps on flowing to you so be open to seeing and receiving it. When you connect to gratitude, you are connected to God.

FEELINGS—YOUR MANIFESTATION GUIDE

Tuning into your feelings helps you know what you are creating. You have a very effective emotional guidance system (your feelings), that tells you exactly what you are creating at any time. When emotions accompany a thought, it carries a lot of creation power. Thinking good thoughts contributes to the creation of your dreams as they will trigger good-feeling emotions that become your creation force.

Think of a bank account. Think of depositing into that bank account. You can deposit $5, $10, $15, $1 million (yes I took a big jump here) into your account, or you can withdraw $100, $20,000, etc.

Now, each time you make any of the above deposits, your emotional guidance system lets you know how you are doing with your money. When you deposit $1 million your emotions are joyous, but when you make a withdrawal from an account that is already low, you may feel some fear and sadness. If you put in quite a few good deposits and feel joyous every time, you create a *huge* bank account of joyous money vibe. However, if you keep witnessing withdrawals that make you shudder, the negative emotion may attract more reasons to feel bad. In the same way, any thought you think about life can be either a positive contribution to what you intend to manifest, or a negative one.

> ### *Your emotions show you whether your thoughts are adding positively to your manifestations or detracting from it.*

There are so many emotions that one can experience, from the highest positives like joy, love, passion, freedom, and enthusiasm to the lowest negatives like guilt, depression, and unworthiness. Then there are many mid level emotions like anger, jealousy, doubt, worry, boredom, hope, etc. While the higher emotions like love, joy, and freedom represent feeling good and in power, the lower emotions like fear, depression, and sadness represent a lack of power with relation to situations.

If you achieve even a small shift in thinking, it changes your current focus and will create a huge shift in your emotional attraction factor. So if you are in the space of feeling unworthy of someone's affections, then shifting to 'jealousy' is an improvement, shifting to 'anger' is even better, and so on till you can find emotions that feel more positive to you.

There is a very simple reason behind the preference of stronger negative emotions like anger, to sadness: it's your prana, or life force. When you feel emotions that are very low like depression, sadness, unworthiness, etc., there is almost no movement of prana in you. Feeling sad is equal to telling the universe that you don't like life and want out, which attracts more sadness to you, and even sickness and other negative events. If, however, you can shift into feeling even jealousy or anger, there is increased activity of prana in your system. There is a burst of adrenaline though your body and life force rushes through to fuel you. Anger is an indication that you are conscious of your self-worth as you are defending it. Of course, if you don't respond to provocation because you are completely sure of your self-worth, then that is an amazing place to be.

Anger, however, while creating a burst of life force also uses up vast amounts of energy if prolonged, attracts more reasons to be angry in addition to having other negative repercussions, and so it is better not to remain in this state. Get out of the state of jealousy and anger, and climb up faster than a jet can take off. The whole purpose of working with the Law of Attraction is to feel great. So isn't it self-defeating to spend time feeling bad? Get onto the runway and zoom into the skies of feel-good happiness! When you are able to feel good consistently, you become free to enjoy life. Your aim should always be to feel good. For every thought that you have and give importance to, observe your feelings and ask this question: Do I feel good?

A simple smile that comes across your face tells you that you are creating something good.

When you feel good consistently, inspite of negative situations, you become free to enjoy life and create your destiny. Soon, the happenings also change in their frequency and nature, and become aligned with your sole purpose of being joyful. You become free to enjoy life. Things are no longer your 'fate' as you now have the power to create your own good fortune, which brings us to an important question; is your future determined by destiny or does freewill have a say?

Chapter Eight

~

Destiny and Free Will

"With my free will I create my future while I accept what has already happened, as the past."

The question that people like to ask is: "Is everything destined, or do we have free will?" Here is something that your mind can play with:

At the level of the Self, you have complete freewill, but at the level of the personality things are destined until you realize who you really are.

At the level of God and Creator, represented by the core of you which is totally into its God nature, you have complete free will to decide the course of your life experience, but at the level of the personality where you are subject to nature's forces, you will end up reacting to these forces according to your personality, and things become destined, until you make an inner change.

DESTINY

As you walk the corridor of life, you see many things, many pictures that you toss around in your mind to find out whether you enjoy them and would like to experience them. As you choose one of the images and lend it your attention, you start to create your destiny. Each choice you make has several offshoots from it and several more choices become available to you. As you walk the path of your choices, you see your future form in front of you.

The picture you choose for your future and your ability to see it through depends upon your personality, which is empowered by its useful skills and disempowered by its negatives. In addition to your own ability to see things through, the vibration of your energy has its own attraction factor, which either rallies forces to your advantage or disadvantage.

Basically, your destiny depends upon:

1. **Personality choices-** For example, a man may want true love and is instead trapped with someone he is bound to by circumstances, just because he does not have the courage to choose what he really wants. His desire for true love is difficult to manifest as he is bound by his nature which finds it hard to be open and move towards his real joy. His personality therefore may force him to make choices that do not serve him well, unless something changes in him.

2. **Personality abilities-** Many times people are not skilled enough or do not have the nature that enables them to carry something through to fruition. For example, someone who has a bad temper or loves isolation may end up unmanifesting his love relationships quickly, thereby determining his destiny.

3. **Alignment of forces-** Based on your vibrations, the Law of Attraction brings situations to you to deal with. The situations may not be what you intend to create. You are vibrating something while wanting something else, creating a destiny for yourself that is not what you intend. Here, the universal forces are not aligned with the picture that you want.

Destiny is thus created by who you are and your choices, attraction factor, and abilities. After seeing something happen many times, reacting to it according to your nature, and creating consequences for yourself, you start to believe that you are fated to live a certain way. Soon you start to lose enthusiasm for life. It is when you are able to be in the space of conscious choice and deliberation that you can choose to change what could have been your fate had you continued to think and act in the same way as before. You can then create a new destiny for yourself just by tweaking some aspects of your personality to effect change in the outcomes you witness.

Free will

Your Core Self does not have fears and knows of its boundless nature. It knows that it is free and beyond death and destruction. In the space of your Core Self, you are free to do whatever you want, lose whatever you want, and even leave this body if you so choose. You are free to spin the contents of your dreams and do whatever you wish with this life, and every other life your Self chooses. Your Self is not bound by personality issues and always gives out clear and confident vibrations, free of fear. It is God power itself and knows that it is the true Creator of everything. Even the Sun and Moon are subject to its power, as are all the other elements of this universe.

If you are able to stand still and connect to this core, you can exercise true free will. When you bring your Self into your life, you can work with its powers and become free of fear, and free to intend.

Free will happens when you are able to stand still, make choices, and see them through to fruition without being pushed by situations and your personality fears. When nature itself works with you because you are connected to Source, then magic happens. Your will is free to play.

For example, someone who knows that he is trapped with a highly emotional and rude woman may be able to connect to connect to Source, stand still and choose differently. He gets into the position of free will as he gives power to the joy that he feels when thinking of being in love with the right person, someone that he knows he loves and will be good for him, instead of settling for the person he is tied to because of circumstances.

The other person who is generally bad tempered may be able to finally stand still, observe himself, and choose to behave wisely and in alignment with his true peaceful nature, freeing himself to see his dream through to fulfillment. He wins right then and there when he is able to be the observer of the situation and act accordingly, not being fooled by external appearances of situations.

> *Every time you are able to do something from a space that is free, you are exercising your free will.*

DESTINY AND FREE WILL

Now, let's make this even more complicated. Ready? Destiny and free will are actually a combination pack and are complementary to each other. The journey is also about getting from a place of 'fatalistic destiny' to a place of 'worshipful freewill,' and that's when the Law of Attraction really starts working to your advantage.

There are countries and societies in this world that are embroiled in fate and fatalism, and they believe that everything is pre-destined with no possibility of change. The opposite to this stream of thinking are nations that believe that they can control everything. They are so much into their free will that they feel as if they could change everything and go to extreme measures to do so. Neither is completely right, and yet each one does have a hold of some part of the truth. Their only problem is that they make it their whole truth.

History is full of such examples. We have invading countries that rule and loot other countries, taking what they can just so they can fill their coffers and feel empowered. They invade countries, rob land and convert people into their religion. Then there are those countries that stay put and allow themselves to be plundered, blaming it on their fate. You can see fatalism and extreme control within the same country itself, amongst its diverse people.

People who like controlling everything, and nations who expend their power controlling other countries are not really acting in free will; they are merely reacting to their ego natures of being controlling and in need of finding external sources of power. Those who think that they are acting in their free will are reacting to situations themselves, whether genuine or just revenge or greed-driven. Either way, they are not exercising free will until they can stand still, observe themselves, and take action from the space of love and true inner power.

Those who believe that it is their lot to suffer and just walk the path pre-destined for them should also understand that when they find their inner power, they too can exercise free will. Empowered internally now, they can see their world change around them as all forces align to work with them.

In the absence of fear, external forces lose their grip on you. Until then, you are ruled by fatalistic destiny.

As one understands that it is not all about control, or the other extreme, of being subject to fate, one can move from the space of fatalistic destiny toward worshipful free will. Why worshipful? Because respect for this universe, should be present in all choices made from the exercise of free will. This will ensure that the choices will benefit you and make you happy long term.

Connect often to your true nature, Source, and you will be in the position of exercising free will from the space of absolute wonder for this amazing universe, projected from within you, your Core Self. Empower yourself by discovering who you really are.

Know yourself and you will know this fascinating universe.

PART II

Knowing Yourself

*"Even if I spend many lifetimes in seeking, it
still is not enough to know myself fully."*

Chapter Nine

~

God and Creation

"I am Source energy born to experience love. I experience love joyfully."

THE BEGINNING

In the beginning all that existed was pure consciousness. Being conscious, it was aware. It contemplated itself and noticed that all it did was 'be' and was nothing (no thing).

It wanted to experience, and so with the power of its thought it started creating by generating and mobilizing energy. Using energy it created many forms; it created the planetary systems, life, and all that now exists.

But what was the reason for its creations? What did the One Mind want to experience?

The One Mind wanted to experience itself, and the best way that it could do this was by playing different roles with its own creations. To experience oneself as a sister, one must have a sibling; to experience oneself as a boss, one must have subordinates.

It started experiencing life in all of its dualities with different emotions, from the extreme negatives of depression, to the most beautiful and positive of all—love. In love itself, it experienced different types of love through different types of relationships. The One Mind experienced love as a parent, a child, a spouse, a lover, love for nature, for animals, for art, for science, for comfort, for wealth, and the highest form of love, divine love.

The One Mind, after contemplating itself, found that since it had the power to create, preserve, and destroy/transform its own creations, it could also be the God of its creations and enjoy the love of its creations for itself. The All, the Divine God, could be experienced as omnipotent, omnipresent, and omniscient, a power greater than all, with a vibration that was purer and higher than all else. The love for God would surely be greater and purer than any other kind of love. Free of negatives, this love would be a source of happiness, and would be called divine love, expressed through devotion. If this love was brought to God's creations, then even familial and other relationships would flourish with the joy of divine love.

> *The feeling of pure devotion would arise in the hearts of men toward the All, bringing peace and happiness to all who bathed in its joy.*

So who or what is God?

The word *God* is commonly known to stand for Generator, Operator, and Destructor.

- ✦ The Generator aspect of God is Brahma, the Creator.

- ✦ The Operator aspect of God is Vishnu, the Preserver.

- ✦ The Destructor aspect of God is Shiva, the Destroyer of darkness.

God is the very same consciousness that created everything that you see and perceive. You can either see God as the Creator, separate and distinct from his creations, or you can see God as the whole consciousness, taking different forms, not separate and distinct from that which he intends. Seeing God as the whole consciousness suits mankind the most, because if all of creation is infused with the consciousness of God, at any time you are always dealing with an aspect of God and are never lost or separate from him.

Within the realm of God, the various sub-gods, divinities, and other heavenly beings were constituted, each having particular traits and powers and in charge of certain universal areas of operation, ensuring their smooth functioning. They are known as gods in some countries and by different names in others, each embodying certain aspects of God. In actuality, each divinity is God, the All, and in that particular form and with that particular name, it represents a particular energy. For example, the concept of the Sun God means that the power of the Sun is regulated by this divinity, the giver of light. By praying to the Sun God, one will be able to access the attributes of the Sun, which is the destroyer of darkness, and seek its blessings. Whether each divinity is the All, or a part of the All does not matter. It is all man's classification to help him work with the universe. Ultimately it is all One.

BEING GOD

In life, we are all being God in one way or the other. We create, preserve, and destroy all the time. This cycle of creation, preservation, and destruction has been going on forever in nature.

A mother exemplifies godliness. She gives birth (creator), brings up her children (preserver), and then destroys the darkness in them (destroyer) with knowledge either given directly or through the teachers she employs.

Here, the destruction is just transformation from one state to another. For example, when there is destruction of ignorance, there is transformation to enlightenment. From thinking that one is just this body to becoming aware of one's true, infinite nature, which is spirit, is a transformation that is a blessing.

To continue in the above vein of thought, a businessman also shows his power of God when he establishes, runs, and constantly transforms his business. In our lives, we buy homes; we furnish and maintain them, and then maybe sell or transform them into another form. An artist creates. A builder creates. We are all creating, maintaining what we create and transforming them into some form or the other, be it money or some other asset.

> *All of creation is but a projection from the one mind of God. Anyone who connects to his core will experience his God power, as it is God who has taken all forms, and it is God who lives within you.*

Who amongst us is not being God? Get into your God nature now. You are not just a personality; you are that, and much more. One does not have to throw off the physical body to experience one's divinity, or heaven, it can be done right now, right here, in the body that you have. All you need to do is to connect more with who you really are.

Chapter Ten

~

The Soul and the Self

"I am a child of God. I am a part of God. I am God."

The soul is basically a focused point of consciousness experiencing life. In the smaller context, it is limited to the focused point, but in a larger context, it is the Self, the All that pervades everything. You can either see yourself as a personality, a focused point of consciousness, or the All.

What you see yourself as, you experience, and this reflects in your manifestations.

The soul spark has many layers to it. At the core it retains its God nature, and at the outermost layers it vibrates closer to its physical nature.

Truth is manifold and varies from case to case, and as you read the Soul-God theories given below, it will become clear that how you understand the soul depends entirely on whether you believe the material world to be different from the spiritual world or whether you believe it to be one and the same.

If you prefer to believe that the material world is made of stuff different from the spirit world, then you can go with the theory that the light of the individual soul enters the human form and infuses the material body with its life-giving energy. If you believe that the spiritual and material worlds are the same, then you can go with the theory that the soul just projects the body and is not separate from it. The soul energy, which is pure consciousness, is fine and pure at the core and gets denser closer to the physical world. What you believe greatly helps in your manifestation abilities. If you believe that the soul projects your mind, body, and your world, rather than just entering a body and occupying it, you will find it easier to manifest good health and wonderful opportunities in your life, as you know that your soul will just change energy to project what you want. Things will just reorganize around you, and you will spend much less time worrying about the material world. You will find it much more lucrative to go back to your inner world and just tweak it a little bit so that what is projected around you changes. Sounds so much easier, right?

> *It is only to have a full life experience that a distinction is made by the God Self between its personality and who it really is—the All.*

THE PERSONALITY

Closer to the physical world, the soul displays consciousness that is more dense and physical, and this physical mind-level soul-energy reflects the actual thoughts and personality traits of the person. The personality is the nature, traits, and physical, mental, and emotional characteristics of the person which are particular to the person, and includes the ego element that gives it the identity of 'I,' allowing it to think that it is separate from the rest of creation, thus enabling it to have a unique individual experience. Needless to say, this has its pros and cons.

The Higher Self

As the soul energy moves away from the manifested physical world and into itself, it becomes purer and purer. It is free of the ego-mind and very aware of its true nature. This is the Higher Self, known as the God Self. At this level, it is everything, and hence has no fear. It is by connecting to this level of existence that universal consciousness can be experienced. This Higher Self is connected to everyone and everything and free of physical resistances; one can *be* everyone and everything. Manifestation is at its best at this level.

> *The key to living life well is to live in conjunction with the Higher Self and to become more like it. As one gets closer to the Higher Self, adopting its divine nature, one also gets its power. Soon you will start thinking like it, as its power infuses you.*

Your universe is but a reflection of you, and as you become more like your Higher Self, your universe changes. As your mind becomes clear and beautiful, free from the grains of sand making it coarse and hard for people to touch and feel, your pure and clean mind is reflected in the faces of all who experience it. Your world becomes perfect. Your world is perfect because your inner world is happy.

Soul-God theories

There are three main fields of thought about what a Soul is vis-à-vis God:

1. **Dvaitha or complete dualism** (God and you are separate and distinct)

    This theory is called *Dvaitha*, or the theory of duality. Here, two exist—God and you. Under this theory, all souls and material elements are just creations of God, separate and distinct from him.

According to this theory, you are God's creation and separate from God. This theory basically focuses on God being a personality separate from his creations. He exists outside of creation and observes and directs it much like if you had a toy train station and sat outside of it, operating it and deciding what goes where, etc. The best relationship that you can have with God under this system is that of a devotee or a child with his parent (not that it is less in any way because you feel so taken care of).

2. **Partial duality** (You are a spark of God)

    According to this theory, God is the Whole and you are a spark or a part of the Whole. This theory makes one feel closer to God's nature by having the attributes of God. All souls together form God under this theory, and each soul is a drop in the ocean of God, having the qualities of God but to a lesser degree.

    For example, a drop of water is made up of the same stuff as the ocean. Being a part of the ocean, the drop has the same attributes as the other molecules of water and can achieve wonders when it works together with the rest of the ocean. The only flip side is that since it is but a drop in the ocean, it is not powerful on its own and has to work with the rest of the ocean. It always has to know its position vis-à-vis the ocean to get anywhere. Yet, there is a feeling of oneness with this ocean of which it is a part, and when united with this ocean, magic can happen!

3. **Advaita** (You and God are one)

    This theory is the most powerful as it brings to your awareness the fact that you are God, and there is nothing but you. You are the only soul; you are the One Mind; you are the All; you are Brahman; you are everything. All of creation is only a projection of your soul. Here the soul is seen in its most expanded version, as the Self/All.

This is *Advaita*, or non-duality. This theory sees no distinction between you and God and is the most empowering of theories, because you are everything and nothing exists outside of you. One who realizes this truth is in his God power.

> *Depending on the state of your consciousness and the level of your awareness, you can experience God in any way that you want—as separate and dependent on him, as a part of him, or as him.*

You can live in any state of consciousness according to what feels good to you at the time. You can also move from one level of thinking to another as you wish, and as you are able to. Sometimes you may feel as if God were separate and distinct from you, a super-power that you can pray to. You feel good when you think of God as somebody who is there for you, taking care of you, like a parent takes care of a child. Thoughts of being a spark of God, much less God himself, are far from your mind and not very real and believable, and it is comforting to know that you can run to God and rest your head on his kind lap. At the level of the human personality, people do tend to hold themselves as separate from God, and so the theory of dualism holds true in life everywhere. When you feel vulnerable in your physical body and it is difficult to believe that you yourself are God, this theory holds great comfort.

Sometimes though, you may find it easy to believe that you are a part of God and are made up of the same stuff as God. After all, if you believe that you are spirit and God is also spirit, then you are made up of him. You feel more powerful when you think of the whole unit, being a part of the whole unit and feeling one with it. This is where you are in the state of partial dualism. You can see it in operation when you observe how this planet works, and the wonders that are possible when people work together as a team, as one. Reminding yourself of your oneness with the rest of this world brings about a sense of unity, and reduces the feeling of being alone in this vast ocean of humanity. After all, no man is an island.

Advaita (non-dualism) can be experienced in activities that bring you into your God hood. This state is more easily experienced by the deliberate practice of uniting with the Self, and is lived by people who regularly experience themselves as God in states of deep contemplation and in life.

Some of these people bring this knowledge of being God into their physical world and live it. They live in this consciousness level where they know that only they exist and that everything is but a projection of their own minds. When a person evolves, he goes from total dualism to pure non-dualism, where he becomes aware that only he exists and nothing else. At this stage, he is God and he is everything and everyone. Nothing and nobody exists but him. He is all forms simultaneously playing the game of life. He is time. He is space. He is everything. Aware of this truth of being God, he may then play the game of life as per his life purpose.

From the point of manifestation, who has the advantage?

Why, the person who is situated in pure non-duality, of course! For a person situated in pure non-dualism and living on the level of being God himself, it is very easy to think of something and it happens. Such a person is a true Master Manifester.

Don't worry, wherever you are, know that there is an approach that will work for you. Meanwhile, you can always work toward experiencing Advaita. Keep moving toward your God Self and start to know it as a definite truth in your life. The benefits are plenty.

Chapter Eleven

Gunas

"As I change myself, my world changes around me. All I have to do is to be my True Self, free of worries, located in sattva/light."

What is guna?

Guna is a Sanskrit word, translating roughly into 'nature.' It includes the traits, qualities, and characteristics that make up a person's nature. When change happens, there is transformation from one guna to another.

There are three main categories of nature that people fall into: the nature of light, the nature of passion, and the nature of inertia. All three natures exist at the same time in one person, and at any moment one of these natures is prominent while the others are less evident. Most people live their lives acting from their dominant nature, though this nature itself might change with age and experience. Acting from a certain guna creates consequences. Let's look at these three gunas in more detail, because knowing what guna you are at any time will help you shift it to your advantage, changing the consequences that you attract back to you.

There are three main types of natures, or gunas:

1. *Sattva,* or light; the qualities of light, goodness, creativity, peace, and love.

2. *Rajas,* or passion; the qualities of fire, power, passion, and lust.

3. *Tamas,* or inertia; the qualities of darkness, rest, inertia, inactivity, ignorance, dullness, and disinterest.

Sattvic guna

People with the *sattvic* guna are basically peaceful in nature and don't need constant fire and excitement to be happy. This quality brings contentment and is considered harmless to society. The quality of sattva lies behind most of life's delightful art work that soothes the mind. People who paint angels, trees, and sunshine are located in sattva when they create. People who are visionaries and think pleasant thoughts for this world are people of a sattvic nature because their thoughts are aligned with peace and love.

There is no downside for this quality except for when a person is in sattva and does nothing. For example, an artist who envisions a scene must also generate enough energy and action to actually paint the picture and bring it into physicality. So this guna must be combined with the right proportion of *rajas* (passion) to make it useful to this world. For example, I may contemplate this book in states of sattva, but I have to have enough rajas to actually write it, market it, and take it to the people. The passion should be of a sattvic nature to help create and not destroy. The energy behind any passionate activity must be sattva, which is peace, love, and light intending to help life and mankind with loving intention toward all.

Rajasic guna

People who are mainly *rajasic* in nature are driven by fiery passion. The upside of this quality is that these people are movers and shakers. A certain amount of rajas is required to get anything done.

The downside of this trait is that when people are predominantly passionate, they can go over the edge, keep trying to conquer, and live lives full of red-hot passion and stress. They can't just be content in themselves. They need constant excitement from external sources and don't recognize that true joy is derived from within. There are many people in this world who are in darkness, and use the power of their words to get people to participate in harmful activities. The quality of rajas can also belong to nations, religions, and societies as a whole, and not just individuals.

TAMASIC GUNA

The quality of *tamas* is that of inertia. Inertia is good from time to time, because being in constant activity is tiring to the body and mind and thus some tamas is required in order to rest. The downside of too much of this quality is dullness, ignorance, and an unwillingness to do anything. People who belong to this group display laziness of the mind and body. Better than tamas is rajas, which at least has one moving and doing something (as long as it is not destructive to self or others). Rajas backed by sattva is good, but when backed by too much tamas causes dullness of the mind and bad judgment.

Depending on one's guna, people experience emotions and display different types of behavior. One who is mainly sattvic in nature will experience more periods of happiness and contentment, and his choice of activities reflects his happiness. A person who constantly has passion flowing through his body may display fiery and passionate responses to most situations. Great anger can be the playing field of one who is located in rajas, since passion can either be constructive or destructive. One who is placed in tamas will experience sadness, depression, and other such feelings that come from so much dullness that he is unable to shake off his lethargy and do anything about it. One located in tamas will put himself into situations that create more tamas and cause for sadness. His thoughts will be filled with laziness, and he will give into dullness more often than not. When one is in dullness with thoughts full of sadness, what happens? His emotions will be sad, as will his manifestations.

> ### *The best choice is to be in sattva with just the right amount of rajas to do work and feel passion for life, and a bit of tamas to rest.*

When you are feeling down and in inertia, lift yourself up with some good music, or other healthy activity. Passion is required, but correct doses of it, not to the extent of creating too much restlessness in you. However, if you find that you are too good and saintly to your own detriment (as in constantly sacrificing your own interests for others) it is good to shake it up with some rajas.

> ### *Saintliness can sometimes be accompanied by a lack of smartness and self-care. One can be good in nature, yet adopt a smart and dynamic approach to life.*

The worst combination to have is *tamasic rajas*—a state of restlessness and passion created from ignorance and darkness. The best combination to have is *sattvic rajas*—a state of light-filled, happy, saintly, and dynamic action.

Rajasic energy can be good to burn away old energy that is stale and ties you up. Sometimes a battle is required to shake things up. Revolutions born out of continued tyranny are examples of rajasic action that shakes things up. The only care to be taken in such cases is that intelligence and light should be the guiding forces, and not dullness and ignorance. When action is taken with loving peace and light, the consequence of that action is also love.

DIFFERENT LIFE FORMS, DIFFERENT GUNAS

There are different life forms all over the universe with different types and levels of consciousness, each having a predominant guna or nature determining its shape, ability, intelligence, and emotions.

Within the animal kingdom, even though a wide range of characteristics can be observed, the main fabric is still the three: sattva, rajas, and tamas.

Different animals fall into different categories depending on how soft or ferocious in nature they are.

Different life forms have different abilities to experience emotions. For example, certain life forms like elephants are more evolved and can experience a wider range of emotions. The human life form with its amazing nervous system is ideal, as the soul experiences life and emotions at their most complex. The human life form has a dynamic and varied range of emotions to choose from, not to forget its brain which allows for complex levels of thinking. It is a shame that people end up using only a part of their ability to live life and to experience it when so much is available to think of, to feel, and to do.

BIRTH AND GUNA IMPRINTS

Your consciousness contains memory imprints of past life experiences which help form the personality you are born with. When you leave the body, you take these imprints with you in your subtle body and are born again with the imprints. Your personality nature takes on a form that incorporates the imprints.

Before you decide to incarnate (we are discussing only human birth here), you create a vision for yourself. You have many angels and spirit guides who work with you to create your life journey. You are never alone. You plan your life journey to help you change some of the imprints that you collected during your previous life journeys. The qualities of rajas, sattva, and tamas would have attracted to you situations that would have created happiness and/or sadness in the past. You have to heal the wounds collected from past lives, not only direct wounds caused to you, but also the wounds inflicted on the mass consciousness of which you are a part and which affect you.

In addition to healing wound imprints, there will be imprints of success and joy that you remember from past lives which call you to take birth again and experience the same highs. The memories of making love, eating tasty food, enjoying luxuries and other comforts are very strong contenders that motivate a soul to take human birth again. Another important reason for rebirth is to help mankind. There are certain people who are born just for the sake of raising levels of consciousness through their actions and teachings. They love making a difference in people's lives and enjoy being alive and happy, sharing their joy with everyone.

In short, the main reasons for incarnation into human life are:

1. To balance gunas and change guna imprints,

2. To heal wounds of past hurt and other negative tendencies,

3. To enjoy and re-experience past remembered joys;

4. To have new experiences, and

5. To help others.

Knowing your predominant guna is important as the Law of Attraction will bring you situations according to your personality imprints, as these imprints are a part of your energy vibrations. Your work is to change the qualities that may be detrimental to your life journey and keep those that are useful to you. As you change your negative guna imprints and release resistances to well-being, your connection to your true nature, joy, grows stronger and stronger. As your nature changes, what you do changes and what happens to you also changes.

There is one more important reason for human birth which brings us to the next chapter. Read on.

Chapter Twelve

Your Purpose

"And I experience my Self again and again."

The most compelling reason for a soul to incarnate into human form includes all the reasons stated in the previous chapter and one more.

It wants to experience its true magnificence.

At the level of pure consciousness, the soul is only light without a nervous system and cannot experience the magnificence of its true glory without the useful tool of human emotions. It needs the human body to do so. Emotions add vibrancy to life experiences, and the One Mind experiences itself in life through its feelings. There are so many emotions that the One Mind experiences through human incarnations. It experiences compassion when it observes someone in a difficult situation. It experiences feelings of generosity when it contemplates giving to a cause. It experiences caring when someone is hurt. It experiences itself as a warrior fighting a war for his people, defending his country. It experiences heroism as it saves people from difficult situations. Yes, the One Mind could experience a whole range of emotions as it chooses what it wants to 'be' with reference to different aspects of life.

The One Mind experiences itself through its creations. If you are Trish or Jim, how can you experience yourself and know what you are capable of if all you did was just be? If you did nothing, how could you know yourself fully as a wife, a mother, a daughter, a nephew, or a boss?

So, you create. You educate yourself, get a job, start a company, find a spouse, become a parent, are good to your own parents, build your home, etc. You experience yourself and your creations fully. You just don't create a baby and abandon it; you experience yourself as its mother or father. You don't start a company and leave it; you become its president, CEO or chairperson, or at the very least make sure that you are enjoying the money and power, even if not directly involved in its operation.

In the same way, on a huge level, God wants to experience his creations; the beauty of the Sun, the Moon, the stars, Planet Earth and its oceans, the seas, rivers, people, animals, and other life forms. He created all of it and instead of just sitting outside of his creations like a boy with his toy train station, he entered his creations, or rather became his creations, and enjoys his own creativity. For this purpose, he binds himself to a personality, and facing mortality and disease, he sets out to conquer himself in the game of life.

For the One Mind to experience its magnificence, it made perfect sense to focus a part of itself into a small and insignificant form and be lost in the wonders of its own creations. From the perspective of a single human body and mind, the universe with all its stars looks so grand. The sky itself looks so vast, as do the oceans. The One Mind did not limit itself only to human forms and human perspectives but took on all forms and enjoys all perspectives at once. Just imagine being a small ship on a vast ocean sailing to its destination, facing the forces of weather and still making it, again and again. The One Mind is the sky, the ocean, the human, the ship, the insect, the tree, the money, the land, the friend, the enemy, the hunter, the hunted, the lover, the beloved, the jilter, the jilted, the giver, the receiver, the horse, the rider; it is everything. So many perspectives to enjoy creation from, aha! How brilliant is that?

THE GAME OF LIFE

The Self wants to experience itself in all its glory. With so many perspectives to live and enjoy, it plays a game of light and dark against other aspects of itself. It starts off with some personality pros and some cons and using energy as the mechanism, it goes through life experiences and the process of winning and losing. It learns from the times that it loses, seeks out the truth, and comes into its true power by realizing its real nature. It breaks the limitations of the original personality, and trains the personality to become more of what or who it really is, an empowered being of light and power, with the happy result of consistently winning more, and losing less.

> *In this space of pure light, the soul in physical form attracts good to it and is now in the energy of well-being.*

We've all read stories and seen movies of how the hero suffers, confronts his situation, and attains victory against all odds. There are enemies who are fought and several difficult situations that are handled and won until finally there is happiness. The hero may start off as someone weak and impoverished, subject to the bullies of society, but soon he understands that it is when he is in his self-power that the bullies will disappear. He trains himself to become stronger than the bullies, goes through a mental or physical battle, and wins.

> *It's all a case of self-empowerment.*

Well, that's what the soul wants to do. It plays a game of moving from darkness into light for which it educates its personality. At the level of the personality, people are generally forgetful of their true nature and power. The personality is limited by its weaknesses and strengthened by its positive characteristics. The positive qualities of the personality help propel the personality forward while the negatives push it back. Think of a game of Snakes/Chutes and Ladders. The ladders help you climb up toward victory and the snakes/chutes make you slide down. With your personality pros and cons, you will either climb up or fall down and make your way through the game of life. You reap what you sow through your thoughts, words, and actions. Meanwhile, the Law of Attraction brings you situations that are either a ladder for you or a snake/chute waiting to happen. In addition to situations that test your personality, it also brings you the fruits of your thoughts, words, and actions. For example, as your personality retains its abrasiveness, you will find that you attract abrasive situations, and as you polish yourself more and more into that diamond that you truly are, you will attract smooth flowing situations that are like elevators for you, taking you up. The soul exposes itself to situations and allows its personality to go through training, lending it more of its own true nature.

> *As the personality changes and goes from dark to light there is victory, because what starts off as an underpowered personality soon becomes empowered and whole.*

Thus, the soul experiences itself through the roles that it plays. It knows that it is the Self, that it is God all the while, but the fun is in aligning the personality to this knowledge, because after a period of not knowing, the personality can finally realize that it is the Self and that it was always whole and complete.

Chapter Thirteen

Wholeness

"I am whole and complete now."

WHAT DOES IT FEEL LIKE TO BE *WHOLE*?

In order to experience wholeness, you must first know that such a state exists.

This state can best be felt in states of *Samadhi* (Samadhi is the conscious experience of absorption). Samadhi happens when your mind is completely in the present moment and you become absorbed with whatever you are doing. If you stare at a flowing river long enough, you will soon become one with it because at this point consciousness completely merges with the contemplated. There is no two, there is only one. If you contemplate a loved one long enough, you become one with the loved one; if you contemplate your Self or God long enough, you become one with the subject of contemplation and discover that you are whole and complete in the process of contemplating one so complete.

Wholeness is a state that is devoid of worry. How can worry exist in a mind that knows that it is the only mind and there is nothing but itself? How can worry exist in a mind that knows that everything is in divine and perfect order?

How can worry exist when you know that the Sun shines for you; that the stars have been created to decorate the skies with small dots of light as if to decorate a party with shiny balloons, just for you? How can worry exist when you know that water was created just to quench your thirst? It was created for you and you only. All inventions and medical discoveries are for you and your loved ones. All innovations are for you. Everything is for you. Nobody matters but you. You are that. Thou art that. *Tat Tvam Asi* (Sanskrit for *That You Are*).

> ### *It is only you that you see everywhere; just you. You are the Whole. It was always you. Do you remember who you are?*

Wake up for you have forgotten who you are. You have forgotten the greatness and vastness of your being. Trapped in the personality you were born with and have become, you continue to act and react to nature's forces and provocations in the same way that any other person who is not as gifted as you, does.

As long as you continue to think that you have no control over your reactions and you continue to feel and react in the same way to external situations, you will continue to be the same person.

Wake up and see that you are not this person that you think you are. Inside of you is a star that shines. This star is beyond nature and is beyond all reactions. It is in charge of nature, not subject to it. It is not afraid of earthquakes, accidents, and catastrophes. It is not afraid of rejection and loss. It is not afraid of being in a state of lack. It knows that it is abundance itself. It knows that it controls the very elements that seem to shake the personality.

Close your eyes for a minute. What happens? Are you able to see what is outside of you? If your eyes were closed, you will not be able to see anything and it will seem as if nothing exists outside of you. There is no Sun, no Moon, no stars, nothing exists without you. You are the observer of it all and if you close your eyes, it all vanishes.

The concept is the same with your soul. If the light of your soul is off, then everything stops. There is no world and there is no God. Just remember that it is the light of your consciousness that is alive and projecting and shedding light on the rest of the world for you to experience, and without this light no world exists. For you it is all manifested, for your precious experience only. Even the 'negative' or 'bad' is there only for you to understand your preferences and make your valued choices, oh divine one.

Wake up and see who you truly are!

When your personality rids itself of unwanted qualities and insecurities which give rise to unwanted beliefs and thoughts, and starts to realize that it is the One Mind, it starts to merge with itself. It starts to realize its true nature, and in such realization it attains its true power.

As you start to release fear toward nature's elements, which also include people, countries, situations, and things, you will align with nature and then the various forces of nature will start working with you rather than against you. Life ceases to be a battlefield where you are constantly fighting one thing or another. You cease to have opponents and instead experience everything and everyone as a friend, and they are all there to support and to carry you to your victory.

Your goals become their goals, and they all want what you want, whether consciously or not. They act in a manner supporting your happy dreams.

Ultimately, you will feel like saying to all those who provoke you into thinking that you are not worthy, "You keep on doing your best to throw me off this space of love, and you try every single trick known to mankind to get me to stop loving you, and myself. Well, guess what? There were times when I was deceived by you and your seemingly flawed personality, but now I have reached a space where I can no longer spend even one moment in hate, dislike or feeling unworthy. All I feel is love, and I choose it to be that way. You try whatever you want, and maybe you can shake me off for some time, but not forever. I know that your true nature is love as I know that my true nature is love, and I choose to remain in this space of love. I don't need to interact with you if it is not required, but I know that you love me."

This is the space of divine self-love, where all that exists is love—love for your Self, love for this world and everything that the Divine created. Being 'Whole' is the state of knowing who you really are and that you need nothing to complete you. You are already complete, and in this space the Law of Attraction works to your advantage, as you lack for nothing. In the space of wholeness you choose to work in such a way that your world works well with you and for you, supporting your dreams.

Bring together the scattered pieces of your mind, and knowing that you are consciousness itself, learn to use energy skillfully to manifest what you want from the space of joy.

You are whole and complete now.

Chapter Fourteen

~

Energy and Consciousness

"I use energy consciously to create good for myself."

The One Mind was consciousness itself, and when it found that it could create matter using energy, it started creating and became God of its creations.

When you become aware of your true self, your consciousness changes, becomes aligned with the One Mind, and life is created from this supreme state using very high vibration energy. For all purposes, you become the One Mind and from this position of knowing who you really are, you can use energy skillfully to manifest what you want. Let's discuss what energy and consciousness are from the perspective of manifestation.

WHAT IS ENERGY?

Energy is power. It is the primal living force that exists in and around everyone. All of creation is alive and pulsing with energy. Energy fuels life. Anything that is alive is energy and has energy in it. Here, 'alive' does not mean only that which can breathe or move. Anything and everything is alive; the rocks and pebbles that you see are alive, the oceans are alive, buildings are alive; every single thing is alive.

The frequency at which something vibrates determines the form that it takes. Things that vibrate at low frequencies are dense and look solid. The material world is manifest from such dense, vibrating energy. A soul, independent of its physical body, is just pure light. Once the soul decides to incarnate into physical form, it gives out energy that vibrates at denser frequencies and forms the physical body, the mental body being more subtle.

Everything is energy vibrating at different frequencies.

USING ENERGY

You are using energy in every area of your life. All of your equipment and gadgets run on energy. Gasoline, water, air, minerals, etc., contain potential energy, which through certain processes generate actual energy used to run equipment.

When two lovers meet, what attracts them to each other is the energy of the other person; the stronger the frequency match, the more the attraction drawing them together. Maybe you recognize them from past lives, but since the external shapes have changed the recognition/attraction is primarily from their energy. What brings them together and matches them up is also the intention contained in their energy about what they would like to experience and whether they want to make this life journey with each other either partially or the whole way. If someone wants to make this life journey with you, you will see him change and evolve to keep up with you, and vice-versa. The opposite situation is when you don't like some people (though things can shift very quickly from dislike to like). The dislike occurs because they emanate energy frequencies that don't resonate well with yours.

You can feel positive-negative energy playing even when you look for homes to buy. Other than the look and convenience of the home, you know instinctively whether or not you would like the home. Some homes carry certain negative energy vibrations that don't sit well with you influencing your buying decision.

All of creation is vibrating energy. Everything that you see, touch, and feel to be real and colorful is just energy vibrating at different frequencies, translated by your body's mechanisms to appear, sound, and feel a certain way. For example, when you come across a certain vibration of energy, your body translates it to look like the color blue. A slight variation and you may register it as green or maybe yellow. Your eyes, ears, nose, tongue, skin, etc., are constantly working together with your brain and other organs to give you unique life experiences using the energy made available to you.

> *Just think of the wonderful, integrated system of this universe and the many varieties of energy that God created just for you to experience. Be alive in that energy.*

WHAT IS CONSCIOUSNESS?

Being conscious means being aware.

There is something in you that is aware of everything, something that is experiencing, being, observing, enjoying, seeing, and thinking. It is the 'Chit' (pronounced as Chi-tha) in Sanskrit. This chit is conscious and experiences life as you. Without this consciousness you are nothing; "no thing", which is the absence of a thing. When you reside in the space of your pure consciousness, which is flawless, it is like a healing spa, and as you spend time in it, you are rejuvenated.

Even if you were resting, still, something is awake and watching. It is the awareness of being alive. Something or someone is observing. This is your soul, which being consciousness, is conscious and aware of itself and life. Even if your system completely shuts down, your soul will be aware of everything. The true state of the soul is consciousness and it never stops living.

> ### *Chit is consciousness. It is the awareness that is aware of everything.*

This chit, or awareness, is pure at the very core. It shines like the Sun. Nothing can stay impure at the core of its being. Can you imagine any impurity staying intact in the heat of the Sun? As the Sun's rays extend outward though, it mixes with the atmosphere, takes on some of its impurities, and changes color, even though the Sun itself remains pure and untouched. In the same way, the chit's energy extends outward, becomes the mental and physical body, mixes with physical life, and takes on the various impurities of nature or at least it seems to do so, while remaining pure and untouched all the time.

LEVELS OF CONSCIOUSNESS

Brought down to the material world, each form, animate and inanimate, has a different type of consciousness. Yes, even so-called inanimate things have consciousness in them and are alive.

Even though all of creation—both manifest and unmanifest—is conscious and alive, the difference is in the extent of their expression. The human form has the highest level of expression, and rocks and other such life forms have very little expression, but this does not mean that they are not manifestations of consciousness.

Mountains, though not moving, are alive. In the mineral kingdom, crystals are known to have higher levels of consciousness than other stones. This consciousness allows the crystal to be programmed to absorb, hold, and dispel energy. Crystals can be programmed to hold energy levels in rooms, and so they are commonly used for healing. Consecrated crystal idols installed in the temples of India hold the holy energy generated by the mantras (a mantra is a sound, syllable, word, or group of words that is considered capable of creating transformation) used while consecrating and during worship. The plant kingdom is also infused with consciousness.

In the animal kingdom, different animals have different types of consciousness. Consider a common and much loved house pet; dogs. They have a very different type of consciousness as compared to snakes and man-eaters. Dogs can love their masters under most circumstances, while tigers and snakes are dealt with carefully at all times. Even if a dog seems wild, it can be domesticated more easily than some natural predators, as the dog's consciousness is softer. This is probably because over time, this species received a lot of love, which developed its personality.

Consider elephants. They have very good memory power and can be trained more easily. They are used in some temples to bless devotees, and being gently tapped on the head by a baby elephant is quite an experience. Apes and monkeys are wonderful examples of advanced consciousness and intelligence, and cows are also beautiful.

Everything is conscious as it is all part of God and God is consciousness itself.

It is said that humans have very high levels of consciousness (though sometimes this does seem doubtful). Among humans, the level of consciousness differs from person to person, with some people being more aware than others. The level of awareness determines the thoughts and actions of each person. The word consciousness here can literally translate to mean *conscience*. It is your conscience that tells you whether or not any action is correct or incorrect, good or bad, and whether it serves you well or not.

ENERGY AND CONSCIOUSNESS

Consciousness needs energy to perform. Consciousness without energy cannot attain or achieve anything, as it is just stillness without life.

When energy is directed by the right consciousness, anything can be achieved. Energy by itself is just power and is like the juice in the battery that operates and runs things. It is the fuel that is required to keep things going. When combined with consciousness, it becomes living, vibrant, and intelligent and can take on different forms and do things. It is with the help of consciousness that energy arranges itself into different forms and acts. For example, a car is made of energy (being dense energy vibrating as a car directed by consciousness to be a car) and needs more energy in the form of fuel to be able to run. In order to go anywhere, however, it again needs consciousness. It needs intelligence. It needs instructions, programming and a *driver*. It needs direction.

Even the simple act of breathing requires an instruction to breathe and this instruction is embedded in your consciousness. It is the awareness of the need to breathe.

Consciousness is the intelligence that gives energy direction.

Not everything is infused with the same type of consciousness. The extent of consciousness in a being determines the level of awareness of that being. Consciousness allows you to think, to process, to act, to philosophize. Consciousness determines your intelligence, wisdom, and awareness. It determines your qualities/gunas/nature/characteristics. Energy coupled with consciousness determines your existence and makes you who you are.

Energy flows through you and around you in a wonderful swirl. It contains information. Your physical brain is a highly developed instrument which analyses the information contained in energy, translates it into an understandable form, and gives instructions to the physical body to act. Before this information is received and translated by your brain into language and forms, it is just vibrating energy. Even intuitions and feelings released by the soul are translated into sensory signals for the personality to act upon and for physical work to happen.

People who are psychic and who see and feel angels and other non-physical beings have brains that can perceive and translate very fine energies not easily comprehensible to those who live only by their physical senses. It is how mediums and channelers work. Energy is received and then translated by the brain into physical language. The accuracy of the channeled information depends upon the emptiness of the person channeling it, and his/her ability to put aside the personality during the process of receiving and translating. Of course, some part of the information might still be colored by the personality of the receiver, so it is better not to give importance to the actual words spoken by the channeler during the channeling, but focus more on the central theme of the channeling. People who are solely physically-focused are also receiving and translating energy and reacting accordingly. The difference is that they are not aware of this process, may not be able to translate all energy, and are bound only to their own immediate physical experiences.

Energy and manifestation

When you receive the energy of a particular situation, you either feel good or bad, and this feeling enables you to know where you are in the process of manifestation, and the extent to which you are blocked.

You are constantly being bombarded by energy, and the trick is to make subtle changes in your thinking and preferences which then changes the energy that you are swimming in. As you change your consciousness and tune only into the energy that you want to work with, things happen. Even one improved thought can create a new flow of energy toward what you want to create. Keep changing your consciousness and swim powerfully with the best thinkers of this world. Let your brain receive and work on energy patterns that contain wonderful and happy information that make you feel really good rather than the same old information of sadness and loss, which pushes you back in the stream of life. The ability to change energy lies in your hands, because this energy is flowing around you and through you in a happy dance. You affect it.

Learn how to direct this energy toward your goals with the Joyful Manifestation process.

Chapter Fifteen

The Chakras and the Kundalini

"My energy rises within me as I experience my true power."

ENERGY SOURCES

The human body works on energy, is energy, and constantly gives out energy, which creates a magnetic field around it. The reason that it gives out energy is because it is alive. The projection of energy in a dynamic way is an indication and measure of life. The more dynamic the energy radiated, the more life exists in a thing or person. Energy is brought into the body through various sources, and this energy is processed by the body for its upkeep and then radiated outward into space, indicating the body's well-being.

Chakras

An important means of energy intake into the body are the chakras. Chakra is a Sanskrit word which means 'wheel.' A wheel is round, rotates, and carries a vehicle to places. Just like the wheel carries a vehicle to places, the chakras draw in, carry and process energy so that there is constant movement of life force in the body.

The chakras are energy centers that vibrate so fast that they seem to almost rotate. The chakras seem shaped like funnels, and during the process of vibration, capture and pull in universal energy required for the body to work. The chakras are located at strategic points and are associated with the health of the organs that fall within the purview of those points. The chakras are also connected with the health of certain life areas. If the chakras are healthy then the respective life areas are also healthy, and if the life areas are healthy, then the respective chakras are also healthy.

The main chakras recognized by some well known healing systems around the world total seven, and these are located along the spinal column, though there are certain healing systems which recognize nine or more main chakras. In addition to the main chakras there are also many minor chakras, located around the physical body, with many chakras located outside the physical body.

The seven main chakras are:

1. The root or basic chakra (*Mooladhara* in Sanskrit)

2. The sex or sacral chakra (*Swadhisthana* in Sanskrit)

3. The solar plexus chakra (*Manipuraka* in Sanskrit)

4. The heart chakra (*Anahadha* in Sanskrit)

5. The throat chakra (*Vishuddhi* in Sanskrit)

6. The forehead chakra or the third eye (*Aagnya* in Sanskrit)

7. The crown chakra (*Sahasrara* in Sanskrit)

Your chakras need to be properly energized for you to be in good health and well-being.

An **under-energized chakra** means that not much attention is being paid to the life area(s) that the chakra is associated with, and indicates a weakness.

An **over-energized chakra** means that too much time is spent thinking of these life areas to the detriment of the chakras themselves. Ultimately, if a chakra gets over-energized, it leads to congestion of energy, resulting in problems.

The quality of your thoughts matter and if happy thoughts are held, the energy of the chakras is light and flowing. If heavy and sad thoughts are held, the chakras get clouded and the energy of the chakras feels sticky, almost grimy to the touch. Hence, think happy thoughts about your life, and your chakras will function well, bringing in good, refreshing, and clean energy to the various organs/parts of your body, essential for them to work well.

The following is a brief explanation of the seven chakras with an affirmation at the end of each to strengthen that chakra. The affirmations help remove fears associated with your life areas, and this helps the chakras associated with those life areas to strengthen, improving energy flow.

1. THE ROOT OR BASIC CHAKRA

The root or basic chakra is located at the base of the spinal column and does the work of grounding a person to Earth. It is associated with the general physical health and prosperity of a person.

Clairvoyants (people who see things not ordinarily seen by the physical eyes) see this chakra as red. A clear red color indicates good health, proper grounding to life, and passion. When people have fears relating to various aspects of their lives like health, security, safety, etc., this chakra becomes weak and pulls in less energy. Its vibration becomes low, with the result that it distributes very little energy to the parts of the body that it is associated with, and must nourish.

Problems connected to an unhealthy root chakra—People attract poverty, bad relationships, back problems, blood impurities, etc.

This chakra can also be over-energized for people who have an excess of attachment to the physical aspects of life, ignoring their true spiritual nature. Ultimately, when a chakra gets over-energized, the flow of energy gets disturbed due to congested conditions and affects the respective life areas, and health.

An affirmation:

> ## "I am connected to Mother Earth, who supplies me with everything that I need for my well-being. I am taken care of now."

2. THE SEX CHAKRA

The sex chakra is located at the space of the sexual organs, and so is referred to as the sex chakra. It controls the desires of a person with relation to earthly life and procreation. Some examples of Earth related desires are desires for sex, food, material assets, etc.

An unhealthy sex chakra indicates problems with appetite, sexual urges, and imbalanced desires and drive. Clairvoyants see this chakra as orange, and a bright orange color indicates a good balance of desire for earthly pleasures. Orange is the color of the flame of desire, lit up and working well, fueling creation.

When people have low drive, it affects various aspects of their lives like childbirth, a happy sex life with one's partner, and work and career prospects. Fear and a lack of enthusiasm for the various aspects of earthly creation is the result of an under-energized sex chakra.

An over-energized sex chakra has the opposite problems. People with over-energized sex chakras are loaded with desires, and are unable to feel full and happy, seeking addictive items like too much alcohol and/or drugs.

On the level of the body, the sex chakra controls the health of organs like the sex organs, uterus, bladder, and rectum.

When a person's sex chakra is not healthy, it looks dull and dirty. A lot of negative energy is attracted to this chakra because of negative thoughts, which further obstructs the natural and healthy working of this chakra.

An affirmation:

"My appetites are well balanced.
I fully enjoy my life now."

3. THE SOLAR PLEXUS CHAKRA

The solar plexus chakra is located at the solar plexus, which explains its name. It is the power house of a person and is associated with the extent of self-power that a person feels in life.

Clairvoyants see this chakra as yellow, like the Shining Sun, which represents power at its best. A shiny and bright solar plexus chakra is desirable to have as it indicates balanced power.

An under-energized solar plexus chakra gets a person to feel ineffective, trodden upon, taken advantage of, and generally creates a feeling of helplessness in one's life. Feeling flutters, butterflies, and nervousness around the solar plexus area happens because of a loss of power in relation to an event, or life in general. The solar plexus chakra is also the center for intuition, and many people who are sensitive start feeling an event even before it occurs.

An over-energized solar plexus chakra reflects an extremely dominant nature that just likes to control everything and everyone. There are many invaders and power-hungry people who have a really dominant streak and cannot be happy unless they are walking over someone else. Such people, even though dominant in nature, are really insecure and are just compensating for their inner weakness with their behavior.

On the level of the body this chakra is associated with the health of the stomach, kidney, and other organs in the abdomen. Since it is located in the mid area, it is very close to the heart region, and so an unhealthy solar plexus chakra also affects the heart and lungs.

A wonderfully bright and healthy solar plexus chakra results in a person feeling empowered, which contributes to the chakra's health, and that of the organs associated with it.

An affirmation:

"I am empowered and I use my power in a loving way. I am safe now."

4. THE HEART CHAKRA

The heart chakra is seen by clairvoyants to be green in color and forms a part of the centrally located chakras.

Like its name, it is associated with the function of the heart, lungs, and also affects the abdomen and throat.

The heart chakra loses its energy very easily when you have grief contained in the heart area. Grief in the heart area also results in a loss of energy from the solar plexus and throat chakras. A healthy heart chakra allows you to feel loved by the universe and all who constitute your universe. Feeling loved in turn keeps your heart chakra healthy.

The heart chakra is a connection between earthly and spiritual life. You can feel love for your earthly life and the people and things that constitute it, and also feel love for intangibles like God and Spirit.

> *Feeling love is a pleasure, and receiving love is a privilege that comes naturally to a person who loves. The heart chakra helps you do this. Keep it healthy and free of grief.*

The minute you feel negatively about any person or situation, your heart chakra starts closing its door to that person or situation with the result that you cannot manifest the very thing that you desire. Fear stops love from flowing, whether it's fear of not being loved or of being caught in love.

Why does a person get highly obsessive about something or someone?

It's because that person does not feel confident of naturally attracting it into his space in a healthy way, and so over compensates by loving or giving too much. Loving too little or too much, as in obsessive love, comes from lack of balance and affects the heart chakra. People need to learn how to incorporate balance in their lives.

Love is a flow and should keep on flowing. Don't let it get stuck either by loving too much or by not loving at all. Confident love is love that flows both ways, and so love freely, but not obsessively to your detriment.

An affirmation:

"I love freely in a safe and healthy way. I am loved in a safe and healthy way. I am love."

5. THE THROAT CHAKRA

The throat chakra is commonly seen by clairvoyants as crystalline (like clear, sparkling crystal) which indicates a clean throat that does not indulge in negative conversations. The best type of throat chakra to have is a clear one that sparkles. Some see this chakra as baby blue or powder blue, again representing translucence.

The throat chakra is the center of higher creation, as opposed to the sex chakra which is the center of basic creation activities. The throat can be used for communication of higher spiritual truths, poetry, song, etc. From the throat can spring the words of a self-realized person, a person who glorifies God and nature itself.

Just imagine what your throat can be an instrument for!

+ From the throat can spring words of love toward your beloved or toward your parents, siblings, and children.

+ From your throat can spring words of love toward your fellow mankind, nature and God.

+ From your throat can spring wonderful lyrics and hymns.

Yes, truly your throat is a divine instrument that represents the flute of life.

This chakra can either be used to express love and gratitude for this wonderful world, or to express sadness, grief, and anger. It's your choice. What you choose to do with this chakra will create a strong attraction factor for you, as your words are powerful vibrations that go out into this universe and become your truth.

A throat chakra that is not well balanced (under-energized or over-energized) can create the need for untruth, hurtful words, abusive behavior and the need to use harsh words (in situations where harsh words are not needed) to push people to do things, over compensating for lack of true inner power. It can also result in coughs, cold, other throat and lung related sicknesses and can also negatively affect the bones of the neck area.

A mild natured person who has trouble expressing his thoughts and desires effectively, may have a weak throat chakra while a person who knows how to speak his truth in a healthy and loving way may have a powerful throat chakra. A powerful throat chakra also means powerful vocal chords and a powerful spirit that sings, and works with the heart and third eye chakras to properly express love and wisdom.

An affirmation:

> *"I lovingly speak my truth now. I lovingly create for the benefit of this universe. I lovingly express my gratitude for this universe that sustains me and everything in it."*

6. THE THIRD EYE

This chakra is known as the third eye as it is located in the space between your eyes and is seen by clairvoyants to be shaped roughly like an eye. For people with a well developed sense of inner sight, this chakra can be seen easily, with open or closed eyes, as an eye-shaped, lavender, bluish, purple-pink whirring disc.

The third eye is the center of your will. When you see a person scrunch up his forehead in focused thought, that thought is being channeled via his third eye in a way that it gets manifested. The more single-pointed and powerful a person's focused thought process, the more concrete are his manifestations. Your third eye is very important and your mind should carefully sort out and channel its thoughts in the most positive way for manifestation. Too much thinking makes this chakra go all tight and loaded up with too much concentrated energy, which puts a strain on your forehead and neck, and results in headaches, neck pains, and shoulder tightness. Relax and take rest.

An affirmation:

"I see the wonderful images of my future clearly now as I happily focus on abundance."

7. THE CROWN CHAKRA

The crown chakra is located on top of the head, the crown area.

Clairvoyants see this chakra as violet-lavender, representing the very pure and healing colors of spiritual love. This chakra is like a funnel bringing in spiritual energy from the heavens, connecting you directly to heavenly love. An open crown chakra indicates that you are open to receiving divine spiritual ideas that can also help in strengthening your earthly connections.

An under-energized crown chakra means that a person is too focused on his earthly life with almost no heavenly connection. An over-energized crown chakra, when coupled with an under-energized root, sex, or solar plexus chakra, indicates that the person is crown heavy, only focused on spiritual pursuits with very little earthly interests. A wonderful balance is good.

An affirmation:

> *"I am open to receiving loving, heavenly communication now. I receive divine messages that make me feel safe, loved and very special."*

The Kundalini

Power lies coiled like a serpent at the base of your spine. It is commonly referred to as *Kundalini Shakti* (Shakti is power). Lying dormant at the base of the spine, the Kundalini moves upward on a journey to the crown, passing through various chakras and centers, activating each one.

As it moves upward it fuels the various chakras. For example, as the Kundalini moves up to the sex chakra you may feel sexual urges, then it moves from the sex chakra to the solar plexus (fueling self-power), the heart (fueling love), the throat (fueling higher creation), the third eye (creating through will), and the crown (experiencing divine communication and bliss).

What a journey!

The various lower centers produce pleasure, yet the type of pleasure and the length of time it stays, along with its benefits, do vary. As the Kundalini travels to higher chakras, the type of pleasure changes from material to emotional, and then spiritual. When energy remains in the lower chakras, it may result in sex but not in love. If it remains only in the area of the heart chakra and does not move upward, it remains as entanglement, high drama, and intense emotions, and does not get transformed into the joyous and freeing love that happens in divine love. Emotional love soon translates into hurt and pain, and even anger and hate.

An important reason for energy to move past the lower chakras to the higher ones, especially the crown, is to experience joy and bliss. When the

Kundalini rises to the crown, there is a thrill that far outstrips any pleasure in life. Centers in this area are energized with resulting physical feelings of joy which makes your head swim with dizzying pleasure. You can take this experience and fuel all of your creation activities knowing that you have just been in touch with the Divine, aka God. In the space of this joy, only joy is attracted back to you.

BLOCKS TO THE RISING OF THE KUNDALINI

If you have blocks of pain energy stored away in your energy centers and along the spine, the Kundalini will find its journey difficult. If blocked, it stops rising beyond whatever chakra it has found its way to. When the Kundalini rises to the heart and finds no blocks, it moves upward to the throat where words of love are spoken, after which it continues its journey to the forehead, the third eye, fueling the will of creation (creating a happy outcome), and then travels to the crown for you to experience divine bliss.

Let's say that you are in a situation where you do not feel free to express romantic love, and carry emotional hurt in the heart area; what can you do? You can share your love with those who are very willing to receive it like your children, parents, siblings, and your own self. You can also pour your love onto God, who is like a cup, ever ready to receive your love. This will help free up the blocked love energy in your heart area. You can also have some energy healing done on your chakras and get immediate relief from the removal of the energy blocks.

> *Don't let your energy get blocked at any center.*
> *Allow it to move upward toward joy and bliss.*

There is no need to take a flight anywhere because with your Kundalini, all the travelling happens within the realm of your own body and mind. The journey from sadness to joy takes place in your own home, in your own heart, and as you remove your blocks to joy, your karma changes and magic happens.

Chapter Sixteen

Karma

"My actions are freeing and attract results that are beneficial to me. I create good karma."

WHAT IS KARMA?

In Sanskrit, *karma* means work, and in order to do work some action is required, which then attracts consequences. In this context, action includes inaction, which also attracts its own consequences and creates more work. For example, if you were supposed to call someone and neglect to do so, this inaction may have consequences.

Even though karma means work or action, the context in which this term is widely used signifies the *consequences of action*, rather than the action itself, that people have to deal with and work off during the course of their life, or lives.

Even though the principle of karma originated in India (though other cultures did/do have their own way of explaining action and consequences), it is now commonly known throughout the world. People everywhere want an explanation as to why it is that they suffer even though they are good. The principle of karma can answer many questions about various happenings.

The benefit of having a belief in karma is that your faith in God remains intact, as you realize that it is you who are responsible for your present condition and not God. You understand what the problem is, that the solution lies within you, and that only you (with Divine assistance if you ask for it) can take concrete steps to reduce your suffering and change your life.

ACTIONS AND CONSEQUENCES

Every action has an equal and opposite reaction, what goes around comes around, you reap what you sow; these famous principles apply to your life because your actions either have positive or negative effects. For example, if you are late for work, the act of arriving late may result in one or more of the following consequences, and each one will set the stage for future actions and consequences:

+ Your boss gets upset.

+ Your tardiness goes down in your records.

+ Work gets delayed for the rest of the day, thereby creating stress.

+ If none of the above happens, at the very least, you will feel guilty and tense.

If you do a good deed that too will result in some consequences:

+ You are thanked profusely.

+ You feel good.

+ The person you were kind to wishes to help you out in some way in the future.

Thus, there is no act that goes without having some effect. Almost all acts (subject to certain conditions) result in a cycle of cause and effect, creating more work for the doer. You cause certain things to happen that affect you. The severity of the effect depends upon the severity of the cause. If you commit a theft or murder, it could have the following consequences:

+ You are arrested, sentenced, executed.

+ You are publicly humiliated, losing your job, money, family, etc.

+ At the very least you spend the rest of your life hiding from the law.

The above lists of effects are not exhaustive, and I am sure that there are more that I have not listed.

How is karma created?

Let's understand what creates karma. Karma is work, which requires some action (remember that action includes inaction). The work required is created by the desire for an outcome, which arises from a person's gunas (nature). Desires spring up according to a person's gunas and predispositions, which depend upon the person's consciousness.

All actions and the consequences are a direct or indirect result of your consciousness. Your basic nature and characteristics influence your desires, your actions and your responses to situations. For example, if you are by nature prone to anger, the anger pushes you to act in manners that create hurt both for yourself and others, thus creating consequences. Through self-help methods, you can be happier, less prone to anger, and less likely to create negative karma. You will be at peace. In fact, this peace itself is your new signature and the universe respects and admires you, bringing you less situations that challenge you.

You must manage your energy system and change that which causes you problems in life—you. If you are too passionate, calm down, take time out, and relax. If you are too lazy, get up and exercise, be pro-active. As you change, this change will reflect in your life.

In fact, let's look at the need for change in a positive light, for example, let's say that you arrive late for work most of the time (you do arrive on time at work at least sometimes). Instead of working on reducing your tendency to arrive late at work, why not just increase your tendency to arrive on time? When you try to work against something, your journey gets tougher, but when you work toward something, your journey gets easier because you are sailing downstream. The ability to arrive on time already exists in you. If you just focus and improve on that, you are doing very well without putting yourself through the washer-dryer cycles of self-recrimination and condemnation. Change need not mean changing a fault in your nature, but it can mean improving some of your already amazing skills. The intention is not to bring in the age-old concept of sin, but to help you fine tune yourself to take better advantage of your already divine life.

KARMA AND BIRTH

When you leave Earth, you leave with only one thing—your guna(s), your nature.

You leave Earth with your mental imprints which contain your nature. When you incarnate again, you come back with a personality akin to what you left with. It happens as follows:

1. You are consciousness, and this consciousness wants to experience life. Even though your soul knows that it is beyond everything, it has experienced life before and wants to experience it again.

2. Life experiences create imprints in the subtle body of the soul. Consciousness is like sticky tape to which everything adheres. This tape needs to be freed of the dirt and other stuff that sticks to it.

3. In order to do that, consciousness takes form again and puts itself through situations that create change. As consciousness clears itself of memories that don't serve it, it frees itself for better imprints that will serve it.

4. Better imprints mean better life experiences.

For example, a warrior will carry memory imprints of bloodshed, victory, loss, hopelessness and possibly strained relationships. His soul will leave the physical body with these imprints unless he changes. If he does change, his soul will leave the Earth plane with less negative imprints and will take another form with a different personality. If he does not change, his soul will leave with the warrior memory imprints and the emotions connected to his experiences, to take birth again in another suitable form, having similar personality traits and attracting life events accordingly, though he need not be born as an actual warrior. The memory imprints remain in his energy, attracting provocations and creating his reactions to various situations.

CLEANSE YOUR IMPRINTS

As life happens, certain events are drawn by the personality's dominant attraction factor resulting from existing memory and nature imprints. Thoughts are generated and the person gets a chance to rid himself of these imprints through self-observation and change. As a person changes these imprints, he gains victory over the imprints that created negativity for him.

POSITIVE THINKING HELPS

Positive thinking is the conscious way of giving power to what you really want instead of allowing your negative thought imprints to hold you prisoner. Observing your thought patterns and changing them will weaken negative thoughts of death, destruction, loss, and sickness until they become redundant in your life. The core of you knows that it is whole and complete and this becomes clear to you as you go through the process of self-change. As you become aligned with your soul purpose, you become stronger. Useful information becomes available to you at the right time, as your soul requires that you rise beyond your limitations, and reach your potential.

New belief systems will create new thoughts. When you believe that people can live longer and healthier lives, you will see evidence of it happening all around you. This evidence may come in as a small trickle at first and then build up as you give it your focused attention. As you start the journey toward your true nature of joy, past imprints in the form of fears may come up for clearing. View these fears as you would view the dust in your home. Clean up, smile, and move on using a positive thought that is more powerful than the negative imprint itself. Realize what needs to be realized in the situation, because with every realization that you have, the past becomes weak and gets cleared up.

For example, if in the past (whether the immediate past or a past life) you fell prey to people's false promises and experienced loss, hurt and turmoil, when you realize this weakness in you, you will work toward becoming strong and self-confident, reducing the importance of the past imprints that became a part of your personality and created hurtful situations for you. The realization brings you a sense of relief and you will know that your karma has changed. You will also have easy access to more positive thoughts that make you feel good, and attract good situations.

GUNAS AND SELF-WORTH

Karma arises from your actions, and your actions are a direct result of your gunas or nature. Gunas are determined by past imprints, and so the key to stop generating negative karma is to change your gunas by releasing imprints that don't serve you, and giving power to your positive attributes instead. In order to have amazing life experiences, it is good to incorporate self-change as a part of your routine. Become happy and light in mind and from this space of light, live with healthy passion.

Your choices make a difference in your life. Having to correct your nature should not make you feel that you are bad; instead, it should enable you to become the best version of yourself.

People who come into your life act as mirrors just to bring out and show you what requires polishing. As you improve your self-worth, your life changes for the better because your karma changes due to the new empowered *you*.

WHY DO PEOPLE REACT IN ANGER?

People react in anger when they feel attacked. Anger also rises when a need remains unfulfilled for too long. The best way to rid oneself of unnecessary anger or any other abrasive nature is to feel secure. Just imagine, someone provokes you with or without intention and what happens; your self-worth is questioned and you react.

Reacting to provocations does not include only confrontational action; it also includes running away and hiding. Of course, anger need not be feared and there may be times when some mild form of anger (not violence) is required to bring about lasting change, but don't remain in the space of anger for long as it is very toxic to you and the atmosphere. Move the energy upward into a feeling of self-worth, happiness, peace, and divine bliss. Soon even that little bit of anger will not be required, as life will really begin to work well for you.

There is no need to fear anger or negative emotions since what you resist persists. All emotions have value, but it is up to you to decide what you value the most. Negative emotions tell you what you are creating in advance, and gives you the opportunity to change your course in time.

EXAGGERATED REACTIONS

Here is where mastering your emotions really counts. There are cases of exaggerated reactions that actually cause more harm than good. For example, attacking someone physically is an exaggerated reaction and can cause such harm that you can never really walk away from it or overcome the feelings of remorse that are bound to come over you sooner or later. The consequences of exaggerated reactions are damaging and lasting. It is how violence happens, the consequences of which may be experienced immediately, or delayed, but will be experienced sooner or later. Similar situations may repeat in life unless steps are taken to change your gunas.

Most actions are not independent actions and are normally reactions to situations, and happen according to your basic nature. Even the act of eating happens as a reaction to being hungry. How hungry you feel, how much you eat, all depend on your nature. Most negative reactions happen because of feeling bad, either about yourself or situations.

Even if you have reacted poorly to situations in the past, it is okay to drop the guilt and work on getting to a space of not needing to react negatively at all. Cut out all possible reasons for needing to react and if you do act, make it your choice. The best solution is to constantly work on your self-worth. Just imagine the scenario of someone completely resting in his true nature with unshakeable self-worth. Wouldn't that be great place to be?

Even if you are not yet that person who has unshakeable confidence, it is okay as long as you are working toward it. Let's face it; most of us are not born with complete self-worth. I know how hard I worked on my self-worth, and I'm the one writing this book! Through everything that has happened and that will continue to happen, keep your smile and drop the guilt. You are moving into the energy of Joyful Manifestation, leaving the past where it belongs—in the past. You are already whole, complete, and very, very loved.

THE CONNECTION BETWEEN KARMA, GUNAS, EMOTIONS, MANIFESTATION AND BIRTH

1. You are born with certain memory imprints from past lives. These imprints contribute to your basic nature (guna) and help determine how you think, believe, perceive situations, and act, forming your personality, and creating karma.

2. Your personality decides your perception of the world, and your thoughts and resulting emotions and actions come up from your perception of how things are.

3. Your emotions behind your thoughts invoke energy setting the stage for situations to happen which creates more karma and more imprints as you register truth the way you are shown it to be.

4. The resulting imprints create the next phase of life and manifestation.

5. As you change these imprints by creating powerful thoughts and adopting beliefs that are positive for you, overriding the negative memories, you change as do the energy of situations, your actions and reactions, the consequences, and your manifestations.

Let the Joyful Manifestation process help you change your karma and manifest your life in happiness. Your joy awaits you now.

PART III

The Process

Successful manifestation happens automatically when you are joyful. This is true for life in general, and also with respect to each life area that you want working well for you. If sadness is a part of your vibration, even though you may have created some life areas successfully, your sadness may affect other life areas, weakening them. When you are in the space of joy, your dominant energy will be joy and will pull in more joyful events. With this joy you can spin the web of your life.

To get to the space of Joyful Manifestation, both in general and with regard to each life area, there are some steps. Even though the steps to Joyful Manifestation are listed sequentially, they may also be used in an order suitable to you, and as required. Sometimes you may need to evaluate, release conflict, and then re-evaluate, and sometimes you may need to empower yourself before you can get out of conflict energy. The listed order does not matter because your mind will get used to working with the Joyful Manifestation process and will become really good at selecting the step required.

The process:

1. Evaluate your universe

2. Ask and Intend

3. Get out of conflict energy

4. Create yourself

5. Remove obstacles to Joyful Manifestation

6. Get into the correct space

7. Create the situation

8. Take skillful action

9. Allow

10. Receive and maintain

The ten steps will help you get to the place of joy and allow you to energize and manifest your life successfully. Let's start with the Joyful Manifestation process now.

Chapter Seventeen

⌒

Step 1: Evaluate Your Universe

"I mentally evaluate my universe, checking the energy of various life areas, and thus I discover what needs to be done."

You are the center of your universe. View yourself as the Sun with the various aspects of your world consisting of your parents, siblings, romantic love, children, health, career, money, country, etc., revolving around you like planets.

Each aspect of your life is like a planet in your solar system that represents either a blessing or a curse, creating happiness or sadness. Just thinking of one of the planets in the solar system of your world can create stress or joy. For the people of war torn countries, their countries present a problem in their universe and peace is just an idea for them, and not a reality. For people facing poverty, it is difficult to cope with the seemingly insurmountable financial issues that may come up with irritating regularity.

In astrology, the assumption is that the planets rule the various aspects of a person's life. The logic here is similar to astrology to the extent that anything that holds importance to you is like a planet influencing your life. For example, if your dog is important to you, it forms a planet in your universe and its health or behavior will affect you to varying degrees. With the Joyful Manifestation process however, you can evaluate the various aspects of your life and bring about fruitful change in them, rather than just being controlled by your life areas and have them dictate your happiness.

You can mentally review each life area (a planet in your universe) to see if it has a charge. If you don't feel good about any aspect of your life, you can work on bringing the life area that causes stress into a place of peace and prosperity in your mind. For example, you may start a business with love and passion, but if it does not bring in profits, the business can accumulate a negative charge. If you want the business to succeed, you will need to bring it into a place of peace and prosperity in your mind.

Repeated stress over certain life areas may result in developing some immunity in order to save the mind, which may result in indifference, so some people end up not caring after some time. However it is not the right approach and it is always a better practice to bring the useful elements of your life into a positive place rather than becoming indifferent and uncaring.

You can work with more than one life area at a time. Some life areas may have a common thread running through them, each one contributing to the others' problems. For example, I had this client who was suffering from health issues and failed relationships. When she felt bad about her health, she could not be her happy self and therefore could not attract a good relationship. After speaking to her, I found that it was the sadness from past failed relationships that created bad health for her because her immune system could not cope with her stress levels. This affected her job and she could not work, which affected her finances.

When her romantic relationships failed, she felt disappointed with life in general, which created negativity and slowly reduced other avenues of joy like being able to enjoy good health, eat good food, go out in public and enjoy a good family and social life. Thus the joys in her life dwindled, and she began to think suicidal thoughts. The most important aspect of her life was now in danger—her precious, God given life.

As we worked to get her to a place where she felt happy and content, she was able to heal her health and other life areas. First, she let go of the attachment to having a man in her life. When she let go of the negative energy she felt good, which healed everything else in her life. Soon there was an avalanche of great guys who were attracted to her joyful energy.

Each life area should become profitable to you, instead of hurting you. When you evaluate the planets in your solar system to determine which ones need healing, you can then follow the Joyful Manifestation process accordingly, enabling abundance to flow easily toward you.

STEPS FOR EVALUATION

1. In your mind think of the various life areas and the people that influence these life areas. Weigh them mentally. How do you feel when you think about them? Do you feel good when you think about a future with them in it, or do you feel blocked? For example, if you think of a possible mate, can you envision romance and a loving married life for the future, and do you feel good about taking the next few steps with him or her? If you feel that there is a future, no matter what the present looks like, and inspite of how it is right now, you do want something positive to happen, continue with the Joyful Manifestation process. Go to step 2, which is asking for what you want.

2. If you don't want the person(s) or thing(s) representing that life area, then let it/them go. For example, think of a friend who continues to act in a way that bothers you. If you don't see a future with her, or at least a near future, then mentally wish her well and let her be. Think of a boyfriend who caused you a lot of stress because he would not give up a destructive habit. If imagining a future with him is really difficult, then let him go with love. Each situation differs and you are the best judge. Just make sure that when you

let them go, you really let them go. You don't have to think about them at all because the thoughts may take you to a place that feels negative. If you do think about them and it creates negativity, then heal and let them go again; it is completely in your power to do this.

Chapter Eighteen

~

Step 2: Ask and Intend

"I freely ask for what I really want, as I am listened to and answered every time."

When you decide to work on a life area and bring it into a positive place, get pro-active and ask for what you want to see happen. First, please get clarity, as it is when you get clarity that things start to really happen, because that's when the real asking takes place.

GET CLARITY

Find out what you really want in order for you to feel good about a life area, or life in general.

So, what do you want?

Do you want someone to marry you? Do you want more money in your life? Do you want more clients? Do you want to be treated with more respect? Do you want this world to be peaceful? Do you want to be healthier?

Again, what do you really want?

Your wants are important to the universe. Your wants define who you are and where this world is headed. If you want more peace for the world, it means that this world will be a more peaceful place. If you want your partner to treat you with more respect, it means that this world will contain more people who treat each other with respect. If you want more money, it means that this world will be a richer place. Get clarity on what you want and make sure that you are floating clear signals to the universe about what it is that you really want to see happen.

A common question is: Why should I ask? If God exists, he should know what I want.

God allows you to experience life, letting your experiences create preferences in you. Even from before your birth itself and right after it, you made your demands—"I want to be more comfortable", "I want more milk!" and moved around and/or cried until you got what you wanted.

The type of asking changes as you mature and get more evolved. You can connect to your Inner Self (your God Self) and ask for guidance about what is good for you. God knows what you should want but he won't impose his will over yours. It is up to you to connect to his will, and not vice versa. He is like a parent who knows what is good for his child but sometimes caringly allows the child to discover the consequences of his actions and desires as it helps in the maturing process. God allows you to stumble upon your true wants in the course of your life but if you need God's help in gaining clarity about what you should want, ask him for wisdom and clear thinking and he will help you.

Just know that the universe takes care of you. From before your birth and after, everything was provided for your existence—air, shelter, food, clothes and hygiene; the universe took care of everything through your parents and society. As you grew, you learnt to do more on your own, including contribute to society. Your ability to make choices improved and you could look after yourself. Yet, with all this self-development, you are still cared for and can always go back to Source and ask for help.

When you decide what you want, and ask, you shall be given. Remember that the universe is not like a bad post office that loses your mail and fails to deliver them. Learn to put aside your doubts, because what you ask for is always delivered.

Ask away!

Let's look a bit deeper into the subject of asking and the types of asking, starting with conscious and unconscious asking.

Conscious and unconscious asking

Asking can be conscious or unconscious.

Conscious asking happens when you consciously frame the words. Conscious asking can take any form depending on the situation. In times of frustration, the asking may take the form of a demand, an earnest appeal, a cry, or even a shout. Depending on the situation, your asking can be colored with mild to heavy emotion, and yes, the heavens have been known to part for the earnest cry for help.

Sometimes emotional asking has such power that the universe moves mountains to fulfill your wishes as you arrive at great clarity about what you really want. Emotional asking, however, should happen very sparingly, with special care taken to come out of the space of heavy emotion as soon as possible, into a space of peace so that what you want can come in. Continuing to feel the frustration of a situation is not a good place to be in, because what you want will be blocked from coming to you. It also does not behoove you to be a permanent tantrum thrower, even if it is with the universe.

Unconscious asking happens automatically from within you as you experience life, without your conscious mind actually needing to frame the words. Not everything has to come into the conscious mind for analyzing and thinking. Your preferences are being known and registered by the universe all the time, and the asking is more of a knowing of what would be nice to enjoy. For example, if you feel good while eating apples, more apples are made available for your enjoyment even without your conscious asking. The asking has already happened in the moments that you enjoyed the apples. Let's say you eat a really sour fruit and do not care for it, asking will happen for sweeter tasting fruits, which are then made available to you. The trick is in letting go of the sour fruits and not holding onto their memory, which would manifest more of the same.

How asking happens

Life experiences have you feeling different things at different times. Most conscious and unconscious asking happens while noticing what is not there or what you have less of. When you notice what you don't have or have less of, an asking happens from observing the contrast. It is called the contrast, because it happens from the place of experiencing the opposite of what you would really like to see happen.

Contrast signifies the opposite of what you would like to experience. Life is very colorful and full of dualities like the light and dark, hot and cold, love and hate, and joy and depression. In your life you may have encountered both sides of the coin many times. Just when you think that everything is going well, the coin may flip over to expose an undesired manifestation, and the undesired manifestation now gives you an opportunity to ask for what you really want to see happen. Most times people are just enjoying or suffering the fruits of their already existing attraction factors without truly understanding that the contrast gives them an amazing opportunity to create new desires. If you already have a good attraction factor for any life area, then kudos to you. Ask that you continue to enjoy and build upon it. For life areas that are not already manifesting what you want, asking from observing the contrast really helps. Creating from contrast means observing what is and asking for what you really want.

Life is about expansion and reaching states of perfection, and nature has been doing it for ages. There were times when slavery was accepted in some places on this planet. People did not pay it much attention and many slaves probably thought that it was their lot in life to be that way. Then consciousness wanted to expand into further purity, and those enslaved felt that they deserved better. This started a process of asking, and the asking was answered. Sometimes things improve smoothly by themselves and sometimes it requires a revolution or a force of greater power, especially when the subject matter touches ones deep emotions and feeling of self-worth.

The process of asking from observing the contrast has existed forever. When man found that there were certain diseases that were dangerous to him, he asked for and received cures from the Divine. Man asked for heat when it was cold, and asked for cold when it was hot, and so heaters and air conditioners came to stay. Earth's whole evolution process is probably the result of a lot of asking from experiencing many contrasts. Just imagine what kind of asking must have happened as mankind evolved:

- "We would like to stand up tall and erect and not be bent over with our arms hanging down." (This is in the scenario that man did descend from monkeys).

- "Raw meat does not taste good. Some process to change it, please?"

- "We're tired of hunting. Can we please have food that is made conveniently available for us?"

- "It takes so much time to sail on the oceans from one country to another. Why can't we travel faster?"

And so the asking continued with rapid evolution still happening. What is required for the asking process to work well for you, showing you positive results, is to not get lost in the contrast itself and thereby perpetuate it, but to ask and let go, allowing what you want to come in. There must be a clear asking for what you want with open intention to receive. Asking from contrast assumes that for every negative there is a positive just waiting to happen. It is important to let go of the negative though so that the positive can enter into your life. Obviously, developing the ability to let go is very useful. Your mind is a very useful tool that can create great wonders for you, but it must first learn to get out of what it does not want so that what it really likes can happen. Shifting your attention to what you really like will actually help reduce your attachment to what you don't want and enable you to let go of it. What you ask for might be just for the time being and you may refine your asking later on, but at least you know what you want next.

> *Your job is to get clarity about what you will*
> *like to enjoy, ask for it, and then let go.*

PRAYERS—ASKING GOD, YOUR SELF, OR THE UNIVERSAL HELPERS

You can ask the All for what you want or you can ask your Divine Self, which is that spark of God localized in you for your life experience. This spark has all of the power that God has, and in fact if you go very deep into this science, it is God. When your personality doesn't feel good about things, you can speak to God or your Divine Self and ask to feel good about things again. You can ask for boons and wishes to be granted. All you have to do is release any resistance that you may have in the form of negative thinking so that you allow good to come to you. You can also ask for new and improved thoughts about a subject matter. When you do this, your Self will help you understand the situation, and once that's done you will have access to better thoughts immediately. They will just come up in you, and you will also find that you have changed the layer of energy that you are in, thereby viewing a new reality.

The universal helpers which include angels, arch angels, deities, masters, and guides, have a say in your life. Each deity or angel represents a particular energy you can call on whenever you need something. For example, people call on Lord Ganesha when they feel that their way is blocked by obstacles. The gods, deities, and angels can help you create what you'd like to experience next.

> *Prayers reach out to touch the universe and create magic.*
> *God cannot ignore the vibrations of an earnest prayer.*

After you ask for what you want, feel good about it and affirm that it is already done. Allow for feelings of joy to now come up in you.

Chapter Nineteen

~

Step 3: Get Out of Conflict Energy

"I let go of anything that makes me feel bad and less than who I am."

You have evaluated your universe, observed what you don't want, attained greater clarity, and asked for what you really want. Now let go and get out of the contrast, because if you remain in the contrast, you will only perpetuate the negativity.

When caught in negativity, conflict happens. This conflict energy pervades your life and affects your joy. Conflict, whether of fight or confusion, is not a good space to create from. When something unwanted happens in your life, your first instinct may be to fight or run away. Instead of being caught in this space, get out of it after taking suitable action if you need to.

Get out of the conflict energy. This is a skill that you have to get better at fast if you want your life to be a happy one.

The mind loves to hold onto things, especially negativity. It needs very little negativity to perpetuate the reality that it thinks is true. Let go of the negativity because most contrasting situations happen in order for you to gain greater clarity about what you really want, and to ask for it.

The mind gets muddled very easily when presented with choices, and it is sometimes difficult for people to understand what they really want. Contrast helps, because when presented with confusing choices, the mind can decide what it really likes, by knowing what it does not like. Yes, it seems to be a rather convoluted and backhanded way of doing things, but such is the mind. When contrast happens, it creates the grounds for true asking and intending of things into existence. Once you have greater clarity, do get out of the contrast energy that created conflict.

Here are some ways to help you let go of the negativity. All of these are similar to each other but I have listed them separately for your clear understanding of each concept.

1. Accept situations as they are

2. Surrender

3. Let go. Drop it.

4. Heal, forgive, and keep on releasing

1. ACCEPT SITUATIONS AS THEY ARE

Well-being starts disappearing when there is conflict in your mind that translates into conflict in your life. When you are in conflict, the turmoil within you is transmitted everywhere, far across the oceans, stars, and galaxies. You start to become a ball of turmoil, and your energy vibrations are now set to attract more reasons for turmoil. Instead of attracting good things, you start to attract situations that you don't want to hear about or see, even to the point of making you want to close your eyes and ears to it entirely.

Accepting situations as they are stops the conflict, and your energy starts to become peaceful again. This is not about accepting defeat but is a way to make peace so that the energy can still and heal. It is easier to create a positive outcome from this state of peaceful acceptance than from the state of perpetual conflict.

In terms of attraction, think of it this way. As long as you are fighting what is, you are actively living in what is and being engaged in it, and then more of what is gets attracted to you. It is essential to stop putting strong emotion behind something that you don't want. Let's say that you feel really strongly about an injustice. Initially, the strong feeling of injustice works like a prayer, asking for a solution. The universe feels your trouble and wants to rush in with healing balm and many wonderful solutions. If you continue to feel bad about the situation, however, the negativity blocks out the healing balm that the universe is trying to apply on you and the wonderful solutions the universe has for you get stuck in the ethers because you closed your door against them.

Strong emotion will serve you in the beginning, but not if you continue with it because the sense of injustice when perpetuated becomes your permanent reality. After the initial strong emotion where you were literally banging on heaven's door complaining, accept the situation as it is, ask for a solution, and give the universe a fair chance to bring you its solutions.

Acceptance helps you get out of sadness and operates like a quick fix. When you accept situations, you stop fighting them, which means that you stop putting precious emotion which is the super fuel that feeds situations, behind them. Acceptance stops you from feeding negative situations, thus depriving them of the power to grow.

> *Accept that the problem exists, deprive it of its ability to ruin your mind, and then allow for the unveiling of good solutions.*

Just imagine if scientists worked in their laboratories crying and moaning about a problem, or in complete denial of its existence; they would be so far away from a solution. These scientists accept that a problem exists, and then work on solutions with calm, centered minds (and nerves of steel, I may add).

So accept situations as they are, and then situate yourself properly to allow for solutions. Remember that a Master Manifester accepts situations from the space of knowing that the acceptance is only a step toward where he wants to go, his ultimate goal of success and happiness.

ACCEPTING OR TOLERATING?

Accepting and tolerating are different from each other. You cannot keep tolerating situations, because the energy of toleration is not good for Joyful Manifestation. So many people live with what they think they can get, and not what they *really want and like*. Okay, this is not to start a culture of non-acceptance or being "spoiled," but it is to get you to look within and ask yourself what you really want. It is about observing what is, and navigating toward what you'd really like to see happen.

Ask yourself: "Do I really like this situation?"

It is very important to keep navigating toward what you'd like to see happen, because otherwise you will just end up resenting what is and attracting more of it.

> *The reason you should be accepting of your current reality is so that you don't end up being in conflict with what is; it is not to make you into someone who has to live with whatever fate dealt you.*

If you end up being in conflict with what is, you will tie up your energy in the space of conflict, which is far away from the space of positive creation. For example, if you don't like the way somebody is treating you, after accepting the situation so that you become peaceful within, take steps to make the desired changes. You don't have to just tolerate it.

The word *tolerate* means "to put up with." Nobody feels good putting up with situations just because they are being forced to settle or live in negative situations. The Self is not at its most creative in situations that it is not happy with. After accepting your current reality so that your energy is not in conflict, take suitable steps to solve the problems. Take back your power of creation by stating what you'd like to see happen. Here is where making a new wish from the contrast helps. Don't get tied up into the contrast itself, but use it as a way to understand what you want.

In life, the universe brings you many samples of what you'd like. Some of it may be partially what you want, some may be all that you asked for and more, while some may be nothing to write home about. It all depends on your current attraction factor. Use discrimination to sort through things and then arrive at what you would really like to see happen. Always remember that you are the localized spark of God creating with this magnificent body and mind. Use them like God would and visualize what you'd like to see happen, into existence.

Even while you eliminate tolerations and navigate toward what you'd like to see happen, take active measures to reduce stress. A contrast that suddenly popped into your field of vision may have you gasping for breath and getting completely stressed.

Release manifestation stress and put yourself into a good-feeling space where every breath you take feels fresh and freeing.

You can accept situations better when you don't have to deal with manifestation stress. As you become an ace manifester, life gets easier and easier, but until it does become easy, what should you do when you encounter manifestation stress?

Manifestation stress happens all the time, even though it is not always recognized as such. Every president trying to improve his country, every writer/actor/artist climbing the ladder to success, every parent trying to bring up children in the best way possible, every person seeking his/her life partner, every businessman/woman trying to make more money, every person trying to restore health to his/her body and mind, and every student trying to get good grades, is manifesting. Glitches may come up during manifestation and it may seem as if the whole world is not co-operating at times. When Mother Nature decides to do her own thing and the forces of the world seem to hold hands against your goals, whatever they may be, lot of stress can accumulate.

Your nervous system and senses are wonderful tools for you to experience life in all its glory, but when your nervous system and senses get overloaded with creation issues, stress happens. Someone with knowledge in the ways of energy can tell you that when you get stressed, nothing moves to your benefit.

Accident and failure rates increase and unhappiness occurs resulting in depression and sickness. In order to get back into healthy manifestation energy, you must stop the downward spiral into negativity.

HERE ARE SOME STEPS TO GET OUT OF MANIFESTATION STRESS:

a. Become still

Drop whatever you want if only for the moment and do whatever it takes to just become still. Take an aerobics class, take up some physical challenge, call your coach, read, listen to mind stilling music, do something (healthy for you). If your body, senses, and mind get completely involved in physical activity, you will be completely in the moment of now, and when you get into the moment of now, you become still. With that stillness all of creation stills just for you, giving you an opportunity to create good again.

b. Realize

Recognize the reasons for your stress and drop them. Understand the stress-creating patterns and let go of any negative ego which has you perpetuating unpleasantness and keeping yourself in stress. Somebody said something upsetting to you? Just drop it because it does not matter in the long run.

If what that person said really hurt and you end up venting your feelings, get out of the stress energy quickly and work on feeling good again. Realize what you have to realize from the situation and let go, moving into happier energy.

c. Start to feel relief

Feel the sense of relief that comes with putting down a heavy stone. Uplift your mood by listening to music, cooking, etc.

Start to feel happiness seep back into your body and mind again. You are now in the process of inviting wellness into your life. Once you start to feel good and well, think happy thoughts of what you want. Of course, remember that what you want must make you feel good. Otherwise, you are calling in just the opposite. Let go of the effort in creation and come back to the space of peace and joy.

You cannot get your nervous system tied into knots. Again, if what you want to create causes you stress, you are calling in just the opposite. During the process of creating, don't speak to anyone who could put your creation into jeopardy. Remember that wisdom is okay, but not discouragement because negativity is not truth, at least not the truth you want to see happen.

2. SURRENDER

As you move from the state of being just a personality to being divine yourself, you may find that there are many approaches that you may need to adopt depending on situations, and these approaches are complementary, not contradictory, to each other. Sometimes you may be in your very human element and may need to believe in the super power of this universe, and sometimes you may be in the space of being the universe yourself. It does not matter, because wherever you are there is an approach that works. In your very human element, you may be subject to forces that may be much greater than what you have already mastered to date. While you may be able to stand straight and tall through most of it, sometimes what you face may be just a bit more than what you have already mastered, and it may just about make you buckle under.

What should you do then?

Surrender to the moment, dropping all doership. Surrender to the Divine and his infinite wisdom. If the situation has already developed, you may just have to weather it like a plane going

114

through stormy clouds. Surrender to the moment and what it brings you. Surrender to the forces, and if they need to have their way with you for the time being, let them. Know that when you come out of the situation, you are going to be stronger and more joyful. Drop all doership and adopt an attitude of worshipful surrender. There is something that you are trying to master in this. There is some element of fear that you carried in you that is being manifested as the situation that you are now facing and the universe is gathering together to squeeze this fear out of you. The fear created the situation which caused people to say and do things to you that you honestly feel you did nothing to deserve. Even though you may already be very courageous and may say and do all the right things, there could be a force that is still greater than you, which is applied on you. Let your personality go through the actions and emotions, but be still at the core, dropping all doership and knowing that the present moment was developing all along.

> *Dropping doership means allowing things to happen knowing that a greater power is doing things, and that you are not really involved in it except to the extent of the actions you are caused to take. You are just an instrument in the process.*

It includes not blaming yourself for every single thing that goes wrong. There could be one negative imprint in your vibrations, and this one imprint could be of such importance that it set into motion a sequence of events coming from that one issue. This issue could be of such great power that it could possibly create an energy field or corridor that draws you into it, making you walk in that corridor and watch every picture that exists in that energy corridor. If you are strong and skilled, you will get yourself out of that space sooner rather than later. For the time being just surrender to the Divine and drop all doership. It could be that your Divine Self is now correcting that negative karma, so just surrender to the process, trusting that all will be well.

Surrendering is the space of saying, "Dear God, I know that I am currently in this situation and would like for you to take care of it." If you feel like crying on the Divine's spiritual shoulder, do so and feel light. You have handed your problem over to him to solve. It's his now. Feel his love all around you and feel comforted that he will help. Call on your favorite divinities, and enjoy the feeling that surrender gives you. You will get the thoughts and ideas required for you to navigate and get out of the situation so that all can be well again. When you surrender the problem, you have to let go of it. Let go and feel the relief that comes with it.

3. LET GO. DROP IT.

What does it mean to *let go?* Why should you learn when to let go and how to do it effectively?

When you hold onto something it remains in your hand for you to continually experience. Any problem that you hold in your hand means that you are continuing to experience its essence, making it your truth and also your dominant vibration, attracting more of it to you.

Many people think that letting go means admitting defeat in a situation. Of course not! It is when you let go of the problem that you can start flowing in the energy of the solution. It is when you get out of the issue energy that you can think clearly, and wonderful ideas float up in you. So even if letting go seems like defeat in the beginning, know that this universe is not here to burry you in your defeat, but is here to uplift and carry you toward success.

Here is something that you can do when you are in a situation that is troublesome to your peace of mind and creates more issues for you; look at your hand and see the poisonous snake that you are holding and ask yourself, "Do I want to hold onto this snake at the risk of my well-being?" If your answer is "NO!", then drop the snake and let it slither away into the bushes. Heave a sigh of relief, pat yourself on the back, and give yourself a big hug. You have just let go of a problem.

Your joy comes from dropping the matter. Learning to let go is essential in order to surrender properly. Letting go means letting God (aka your Higher Self, the All) handle the situation, for it is when God comes in that healing really happens and you become ready to move into a new space. Even in letting go, you can state your wish about what you'd like to see happen. Your preferences do matter.

4. HEAL, FORGIVE, AND KEEP ON RELEASING

The situations that you attract come into your experience because somewhere there is a weakness in your mental body and belief systems. Somewhere there is a grain of fear that exists toward whatever happened or is happening. There could also be general anger, sadness, and pain toward life. The heart chakra contains the emotional baggage of all of these fears, and in fact the other chakras could also hold fear related to the life areas they are affiliated with. It is important to release the baggage that you carry.

Forgiveness helps.

Forgive anything and anybody who has hurt you. If there is no particular person that you can pinpoint, then forgive the world and creation itself for what you consider to be unfair treatment. Forgive your body for whatever pain it has given you, and forgive your mind for not being 'all there' in some situations, and for getting you into tight spots and creating worry for you.

Keep on forgiving until you reach the point of knowing that there is nothing and nobody to forgive. Everybody, in this world, was just acting according to the consciousness prevailing at that particular time. Nobody intended to hurt you. They were all just acting according to their nature/gunas and according to the energy conditions prevailing at the time. Soon you will come to the conclusion that there was no culprit. Since everyone was acting and responding according to the program contained in the atmosphere at that time, who can you blame?

If you want to really put the blame on anyone, put it entirely on the Divine's shoulders. You can tell the Divine that it is he who gave you your personality and the personality of others that created the situation, and therefore it is he who should rectify the situation. This is also a form of letting go, even if from the space of a bit of anger against the Divine.

No problem. The Divine can take it. All he wants is for you to be in active communication with him. Don't be stuck in the anger energy though; move out of it. We all know what happens in the world when people are stuck in anger and revenge. Nobody is served. Putting the blame on the Divine will seem contrary to what I wrote under the topic of karma, where the theory of karma helps people take responsibility for their own energy and not blame God for everything that happens, but it is quite complementary. If you want to change your energy and not be stuck in it (which serves to change your karma), you can use the tool of putting the blame temporarily on the Divine so that you can wiggle out of the sadness in the situation. This is just a tool and not a crutch to be leaned on forever.

When you use this tool, use it sparingly and also with the intention of navigating out of the sad energy where you feel helpless. It is also a message to your Higher Self to make your personality more empowered to attract better situations to you and not keep repeating the same problems in your life. It is a way of acknowledging that you were not fully equipped to deal with the situation, and that you want to be empowered now so that you can attract good to you. It completely changes your attraction factor as you get empowered by saying to the universe that you will not be subject to such situations anymore because you deserve better, and know it to be the truth.

Once you are freed of the need to blame the people in the situation, you are free of the push and pull in it. With forgiveness comes a healing of such great depth that your vibrations change. Whatever negativity you were holding onto no longer exists in your vibrations, which means that the Law of Attraction brings you a different reality.

When you take action based on somebody else's negativity, you may not be right in your own action. The mind loves linking the current moment to the past. Actions based on provocations may be understandable, but may also bring back consequences that you may not want.

If you do end up taking action that brings you negative consequences, release the guilt and forgive yourself. Change the energy so that the situations have a chance to heal on their own. They will not heal if you hold onto them. Truth is manifold and even if it seems like a mistake has been made, there really was no mistake. All you need to do is use the right logic to navigate your way out of the situation. Remember always that everything is in divine and perfect order under the seeming chaos.

Getting out of conflict lays the road for the next step, which is creating and empowering yourself. As you empower yourself, you can let go more easily, and as you let go more easily, you empower yourself more easily. The efficient ability to accept, let go, surrender, and forgive comes from a nature that is connected to itself, to Source, and to the universe. A good dose of self-love (love from knowing your God Self, and who you really are) and an increase in your self-worth will really help. Get empowered now.

Chapter Twenty

~

Step 4: Create Yourself

"The faster I discover myself and become who I really am, the faster my mind is aligned with the Self's dreams."

When some situations happen, or when you think of certain life areas or people, do you feel as if you are losing power? When you lose power, you lose life force which is required for happy manifestation. It is important to empower yourself, to make yourself into the person who attracts positive situations. No more need to fight for what you want as your inner power and complete confidence will shine and be reflected back to you in the mirror of the universe. Your external world changes to reflect your inner power.

To change an external situation efficiently you must be equal to or greater than that situation in terms of inner power.

So how can you make yourself into a person for whom things go well?

1. Discover who you really are—realize yourself

2. Build up confidence—empower yourself

3. Develop a strong immune system

4. Become a Master Manifester, not a Master Unmanifester

1. DISCOVER WHO YOU REALLY ARE— REALIZE YOURSELF

When you think of yourself as someone much greater than just a limited personality, and bring this knowledge to your personality, you become as vast as the ocean and the skies. Your dreams also come from that space, as do your powerful manifestations.

The process of self-empowerment is simple, and yet one of the most complex tasks in this world. It involves going beyond the body and then coming back to the body to create a confidence that is far reaching in its effects. As you discover and know who you really are, you are able to bring this knowledge into your physical world, and that really helps.

> *Realize that you are not just this physical body, but the Self itself.*

Who are you? Are you this body? Are you this collection of senses, blood, skin, and flesh, or are you something else? What are you? Ask yourself these questions over and over again. You will first come up with answers like: "I am Tanya; I am a woman; I am an artist; I am human; I am this; I am that ...." When you run out of the physical definitions of who you are and start looking for answers that are not personality related you may stumble upon the right answer—"I am the Self; I am everything and yet I am nothing. I am consciousness. I am divine. I am. I simply am."

When you arrive at who you really are, or rather at *what* you really are, you will connect to Source/Higher Self that resides in and presides and prevails over everything. Understanding who you are is very important, because it enables you to let go of the drama and really live. As you realize who you are, you serve the purpose of empowering yourself, because you are so much more than who you *think* you are.

If you are a spiritual person, you may already recognize yourself as a point of consciousness focused into this physical life journey. Great! But the truth is that you are much more. You are *all* points of consciousness. You are it *all*. You are space, you are eternity and you are the unmanifest and the manifest all at once. You are the Higher Self which is a part of everyone and everything, or rather everyone and everything is a part of your Higher Self. So if your Higher Self is a part of everyone and everything, and everyone and everything is a part of your Higher Self, and you recognize this fact, how empowering is this knowledge for you? You will be able to live this life seeing yourself in everyone and everything, and it will help your manifestations enormously. After all, if you are the actress and the casting director, it works in your favor does it not? All you have to do is to connect to your Higher Self (which is in everyone and everything) and allow good to come in.

To connect to your Higher Self, just call on your Higher Self with an invocation.

For example: "Dear Self, I know that you exist and wish to connect to you more and more. I know of your presence and felt you guide me many times in the past. I hear your voice clearly when I am quiet. I wish to feel your guiding hand in my life and want to merge with you more and more, becoming one with you. I would like for your qualities to infuse my personality. Thank you."

As your Higher Self lends you more of its amazing joy and power, you realize your True Self more and more. As this happens, more of who you really are shows up in your personality, and you will stop feeling limited by your current physical reality and will learn to transcend it. As you learn to transcend the limitations of your current physical reality, your powers increase, and you are free to fly and be happy. You are free to choose, because you are now situated in your power to ask for what you want and to have it happen. Now the asking becomes more of an intension, than a plea, because you are the Self itself.

2. BUILD UP CONFIDENCE—EMPOWER YOURSELF

Even as you work on realizing who you really are, far beyond the personality that you see, you must continue to work at the level of the personality on polishing and empowering yourself, whatever that means to you. The need to empower yourself will arise on many occasions in your life. Every time your boss fires you, every time someone hurts you, every time you feel as if you don't have enough money or love in your life, every time you don't feel beautiful just the way you are, and every time something threatens your existence, do something for yourself to feel confident again. Just make sure that whatever you do to balance this feeling of things not being okay is healthy and good for you in the long run, and is not self-defeating to your current goals.

Some nice things to do to feel confident:

a. Work out and feel your body become strong and healthy.

b. Eat good, healthy food.

c. Conquer a habit that you have been trying to change.

d. Treat yourself to a healing massage, a facial, or buy yourself something nice, but not to your financial detriment. Trust your feelings, but make sure that you don't do anything that has you swinging from a high to a low in the span of a few minutes. For example, if you buy a dress that costs $250 and it makes you feel good, make sure that you don't swing to a low after seeing the dent in your bank account or the figures in your credit card statement. Learn to balance your ups and downs.

e. Stop see-sawing as it is not good for anyone. From the above example of the costly purchase, the high highs and the low lows take their toll on your nervous system.

f. Spend time with your family and other loved ones and allow the feeling of being in good, loving company to seep through you. For example, as a woman, if you connect more with your father and brothers, you will feel so taken care of by the males in your family that it improves your 'I'm taken care of well' vibe, attracting a wonderful man who will also take good care of you. The same logic applies to the energy of your mother and sisters. Connecting to them creates the feeling of being loved and adored, which has its own positive attraction factor as you connect more with the Mother Divine whose job is to take care of you, her precious one. Conversely, if you are not in the position of having an immediate, loving family with you, shake free of the need to have one and stand tall, happy, and proud because you have your Self, which has been with you forever. Take the approach that suits your situation the best.

g. Listen to music, sing, dance, watch funny movies and entertain yourself. These happy vibes will serve you well.

h. Think of the good given to you by your parents, the world, and the Divine—your eyes, hair, health, any family wealth, etc., and feel happy about them.

i. Think of how strong you have been to survive the problems the universe has thrown in your way. You have crossed them all and emerged victorious. You are here, you are alive, and you are rocking.

j. Think about the fact that you are a spark of the Divine. Every drop of water in the ocean has all the properties of the ocean and just like that, you too have all the qualities of the Divine because you are its spark. All you have to do is to ask for these properties to come into your personality and take root in your life.

k. Be around happy, positive people and connect to their energy. Reading up on successful people and how they made it, allows you to swim in their space.

l. Maintain a success journal and keep track of everything good that happens.

m. Train yourself in the skills required to improve your performance at your job, and other places.

n. Feel good that what you want is happening and will happen.

When you move away from your personality fears and move toward your True Self, you will reach a space of inner power. As your inner psychological world starts changing, it directly affects your external world. From the inner to the outer do things flow. Energy is now fruitfully spent correcting one's inner world and seeing the external world change as a result. When this happens, the need to prove oneself again and again by controlling external factors or by reacting negatively to external factors becomes redundant.

As a person's emotions mature, he experiences more joy-filled states of love, and his tendency to violate other's rights and have his violated, decrease. His mental immune system becomes strong from the practice of self-love, and remaining in states of well-being.

3. DEVELOP A STRONG IMMUNE SYSTEM

Just like your body has an immune system that fights invaders and wards off diseases, your mind has its own immune system. Build up your mental immune system until you get to the place where nothing touches you or brings you down either mentally or physically. In fact, once your mental immune system is strong, your physical immune system also becomes strong.

The stronger your self-confidence and self-worth, the stronger your mental immune system. A strong mental immune system can ward off the sharpest of attacks whether through hurtful relationships, financial drain, insult to reputation, loss of power, etc. Once your mental immune system is strong, your attraction factor changes for the better. Until then, fear in your mind becomes an open target for situations to happen. So if you do have some fear toward someone or something, use precise logic to reduce or overcome that fear, thereby changing your vibrations.

For example, if you believe that someone could break into your home at night, then this fear is a weakness in your mental immune system. Just like you would secure your home, you have to secure your mind against this weakness. Remove this fear from the roots, or at least reduce it. So how do you reduce the fear that someone could break into your home at night? This fear could be supported by thoughts like:

+ The world is full of negative energy.

+ The newspaper is full of such happenings.

+ People are greedy.

+ People don't know how to respect other's property.

+ Only last month someone's home was broken into in our neighborhood.

+ Haven't you seen those boys walking around having nothing else to do?

These thoughts support your fear of your home being broken into. Now, use some good logic that will help remove or reduce your fear. You don't have to convince anybody else; you just have to convince your own mind to be silent, happy, and safe.

+ Many good people populate this world and create positive energy.

+ The police in this area are alert and are cruising around in their cars.

+ The lady whose home was broken into could have carried her fear around her like a beacon of light, attracting the negative situation to her. I am not like that.

+ The doors and windows of my apartment are secure. Even I find them hard to open, and I am the one living here.

+ I use an alarm system.

+ I lock my bedroom door at night, and I could always push a dresser against it.

+ I say prayers and ask my angels for protection, so how can anyone or anything negative come near me? I am well protected.

+ For every home that is broken into, so many homes are left untouched.

+ Even if my home is broken into, so what? I can handle it.

- My dog hears the softest of noises, and his bark will frighten the thieves away.

- My neighbor's dog is always on the alert.

- My apartment complex has had no attacks of such kind, or very few of them. I live in a safe neighborhood. There are after all some advantages to the amount of rent I pay here, one of which is safety.

- I keep a rod under my bed. Nobody gets the better of me!

Do you feel better now? Do you feel a smile of relief coming up? Do you feel more safe and secure? Good. You have just strengthened your mental immune system using a combination of better thoughts and logic that your mind can work with and feel good about. Like I said before, there is nobody else that you need to convince; just yourself.

> *Every time you strengthen your mental immune system, your attraction factor for the negative reduces drastically.*

Other than having better thoughts by using logic to convince your mind, you should also rest your mind and nervous system by strengthening it from within. Just imagine what would happen if your household equipment or your car got really heated up. In the same way, your nervous system needs to cool down from time to time. It's great to incorporate practices that give you deep rest and strengthen your mental and physical immunity, generating tons of good energy.

INCORPORATE HAPPY PRACTICES

Physical activity and some other methods help build up your physical and mental immunity. Incorporate an exercise regimen and lead an active life with a healthy dose of aerobics, weight training, dance, music, and other physical activities that will keep you active, healthy, and feeling as if you are taking care of yourself. Surround yourself with beauty, and a wonderful, free-flowing atmosphere with plenty of fresh air. As you become someone who is empowered and confident, your world will reflect that well-being. This planet is in ascension and people need to create their space of well-being now.

You must carefully select the energies you choose to associate with. Strengthen and anchor yourself to the energy of well-being and from that space handle everything else. Who you are matters, as your creations depend on that. If you are a king, your creations come from that level. If you are the Divine, your creations happen accordingly. If you think that you are beautiful and have confidence, your creations come from that space. What a wonderful way to Joyfully Manifest!

You are active and happy, and the Law of Attraction brings you more reasons to celebrate.

4. BECOME A MASTER MANIFESTER, NOT A MASTER UNMANIFESTER

Consciously become someone who is a Master Manifester, and know yourself as a Master Manifester. This knowledge will really help you in your creations.

A past moment is a past moment and must not become a part of your next moment, which is new and stands by itself. Your job is to become a Master Manifester and not a Master Unmanifester. You should watch your thoughts and actions to see if you are in the process of manifesting or unmanifesting. Some points to consider:

+ Decide what you are doing in a situation. Ask yourself: "Am I in the process of manifesting or unmanifesting?"

+ If you have already built three floors to a building that you want to manifest, then don't destroy what you have already built. Build on top of what you have already created unless you really need to rebuild from scratch and that is your conscious choice.

+ When you realize what has to be realized in a situation, you will change the energy pattern.

+ Others become amenable to listening to you after you change your energy. Things just change around you.

+ When you see trouble brewing around you, intend again that you want to see the situation through to success. Your energy will start getting ready for it.

+ Have one good thought and several similar thoughts will come together and stick like glue, forming a strong vibration and attracting positive situations for you to experience.

+ Flow in the energy of the solution instead of the problem. This will determine which energy corridor you are travelling in and what scenery you view as a result of the space you are in.

+ Use negativity selectively after deciding whether you want to manifest or unmanifest the situation. Don't get bounced around by nature. The more mature you are in your thoughts, the more mature nature treats you. This has nothing to do with being childlike, innocent, and eager. Be childlike and happy in your approach to this world but be aware of what you are creating. A child is not aware of consequences, but you are. Even as you bounce around happily, the level of awareness you have determines your happy life journey.

For example, if you want your relationship to continue working and you really feel that you are with the right partner, give up negative thoughts about it and build up positive thoughts. If you want to get out of a job, it is better to float good energies toward the job that you really want instead of floating massive doses of negative energy toward the job that you want to leave. This secures all your actions in well-being, and you can then take off in your new job from the space of well-being instead of having to prove yourself all over again.

Be a Master Manifester instead of a Master Unmanifester. Even while having negative thoughts, be conscious of the fact that you are doing so, and don't get fooled into thinking that your thoughts are the truth. Everything is fluid and can change anytime.

Chapter Twenty–One

~

Step 5: Remove Obstacles to Joyful Manifestation

"And I remove anything in me that comes between me and my creations."

After feeling good about yourself with the process of self-empowerment, it is essential to remove the blocks to Joyful Manifestation. If the blocks are left there, or built up on, they will sabotage successful manifestation.

To remove them it is first important to become aware of them. When I say become aware, I do not mean the same thing as 'focus on'. You can be aware of something and know that it could be a possible pitfall for you, but you don't have to focus on it and make it your whole truth. Many times just being aware of the issue lays the road for rectification.

For example, if you are a woman afraid that her man is going to find someone younger and more attractive, your enemy is not that younger so-called more attractive person, but your thoughts about yourself. If you are in this position, then read up on *Step Four* again and get empowered. Since everything in this world is true and yet nothing is true, you can make it whatever you want. To explain this further, you can either think that "Yes, this world is full of young and beautiful women ready to take away my guy", or you can think that "I am the most beautiful and perfect of them all." It's your choice; what do you want to think? What is it that serves you? Once you start thinking that you are the best, then even if temporarily you are shown otherwise, you will soon be proven right. You will see that you are the most beautiful of them all and are the natural choice for your guy. Beauty can mean so much more than just pure physical looks; the shape of the body and the color of hair. In fact, the body shape that you have may really be wonderful for all you know. Who is to say what the right standard for beauty is? It keeps on changing. So really the obstacles are always within you to remove, but you must first become aware of their existence so that you can remove them.

What are the common obstacles that hurt the successful manifestation of situations?

1. One's basic nature

2. Past experiences and karmic imprints

3. Inability of the mind to perceive

4. Resistance

5. Fear

6. Beliefs

7. Doubt

8. Negative Ego

9. Lack of confidence in ability

10. Inability to stay in the now

11. Misery

1. ONE'S BASIC NATURE

Each person is born with a basic nature. This basic nature is made up of tendencies to do certain acts, think in certain patterns, say certain things, and react in certain ways.

There are several factors that contribute to this basic nature—birth and genes, family and social conditions, upbringing, gender, race, and individual and mass experiences. All of this contributes to the creation of your personality.

Every species has a basic nature; plants, animals, minerals, etc., all have basic natures and tendencies and they act according to this nature. This nature is given to them by God as it is a part of his creation plan that things act according to their nature. Mountains are supposed to act like mountains and not move around freely. Wouldn't it be something if mountains decided to start walking around, or at the least start sliding around intentionally?

From the variety of species present today on Earth, man is known to be the only one that can most consciously bring about a great change in his environment and in his own nature by virtue of his understanding and will to do and achieve things. To consciously contemplate, make choices, plan and execute the plans is something that mankind can do. All species have their own intelligence to perform their survival tasks adequately, but humans are endowed with an extra ability to stand still (when the mind is calm), think, make educated decisions and then execute those decisions into action. Conscious processing and conscious action allows mankind to progress well.

Every person has a basic nature and this basic nature dictates what he will normally do in a situation. While his actions may work for him sometimes, it may not always work. Even as he may try to control his behavior and actions, when faced with similar conditions, his reactions would probably be the same. The key lies in changing his nature to the extent that it works for him. When a person can sit still, think, and make a conscious change, he removes one of his biggest obstacles to Joyful Manifestation, which is acting in self-defeating patterns. A very simple example is of a person who wants to stick to a job, but can't do so because of his short temper. How will he reach Joyful Manifestation unless he works on and changes his basic nature?

Observe your reactions to situations and ask that your basic nature changes so as to enable you to plan and respond in a way that makes the situation, rather than breaks it. It is never too late to do something that will further reinforce your becoming a Master Manifester rather than a Master Unmanifester.

An affirmation:

> ### "I allow my basic nature to work to my advantage. I allow change that is useful to me."

If something is not working for you, there is no harm in allowing winds of change in. Don't hold on to that which is no longer required by you.

2. PAST EXPERIENCES AND KARMIC IMPRINTS

The memories of past experiences linger on as photographic imprints in your energy field, your brain, and your cells. It's not just your own memories that linger, but also the memories of some of the experiences of the people around you, and the world in general.

Connectivity happens as you associate these memories with people, objects, and situations. Other than the physical neurons that are fired every time you make such an association, there is also a tendency to pull on energy ropes that bring in a flood of matching experiences.

The stronger the imprints, the stronger the connections, and the stronger the pull on the experiences, bringing them into your current world. Somewhere one of the links in this chain has to be consciously broken. Again this is something within man's skill set. If the memories work for you and if you feel good about them, then keep them as a part of your good vibes. If the memories don't serve you, then let them go. Expose them to light, and by that I mean become aware of those imprints. Becoming aware of them will help make them disappear, unless of course you want to build your home on them. What happens when you expose film to light? The photographic images fade away. Use the same logic and expose unwanted memories to light.

Each memory that you carry has a vibration to it, adding to your current reality and what you may pull in later. Release unwanted memories and clean up your disc space. These imprints are karmic imprints and you must work on them, consciously aware of the power they hold to take you ahead, or to push you back.

An affirmation:

> *"I allow my energy to cleanse itself of imprints that do not serve me. I keep that which is for my higher good and let go of others that I do not need."*

3. INABILITY OF THE MIND TO PERCEIVE

Because of the vast barrage of memories that come up with annoying regularity, your mind can sometimes find itself in a maze and be confused as to the truth of any or all of them. It loses the ability to focus on the thoughts that serve it, and just keeps mulling on bad feeling thoughts that deprive you of good feeling experiences. This also affects your perception of situations and things around you, which affects healthy reactions to life, and your intentions. It always pays to learn how to focus your mind correctly on thoughts that serve it. Learning how to choose what to focus on is a skill, and the more you learn how to use this skill, the better your reality will be.

Let's say that you want to start a business. As you research into the nature of the business and how to establish it, a lot of information becomes available to you. What will you focus on? If you focus on the positive, you attract more positive information about what you want, which increases your chances for success in that business. As you learn how to perceive all the bits of information in a light that serves you well, you become established to pull in good-feeling thoughts and matching situations.

Even with negative information, nobody is asking that you put a cloth over your head and refuse to see it. Instead, use the information to get educated on what you can do to decrease your chances of attracting negativity. As you get educated in the ways to think and do things correctly, your positive vibrations increase as fear is reduced. As you learn to focus on thoughts that serve you, you can make your action choices wisely. As your ability to perceive situations improves, your thoughts improve, which then improves your life.

An affirmation:

"I perceive situations to my happy advantage."

4. RESISTANCE

When you are used to getting something easily, you feel good. You know that all you have to do is ask and it is given.

In those life areas where you have had to fight for what you want, you experience blocks to the happy and natural manifestation of your desires. These blocks arise from resistance. Resistances are the result of past situations that created struggles for you and are reinforced in your mind in the present moment by further external evidence.

All external situations are a result of the energy that has built up till date and are born out of your beliefs of how things are, or were.

For example, a son born to very rich parents knows that all he has to do is ask for something and he will get it with hardly any opposition. He does not experience any obstacles in his world (inner or outer) when it comes to the fulfillment of the desires that money can buy. He may not, however, experience this same free-flowing state in all areas of life. For example, in the area of true love he may encounter several hurdles arising from his beliefs about himself, and others; he may feel that he is being loved for his money, he does not look good, etc. As a result of his beliefs, he may experience several situations that actually confirm them, creating stress in his life.

Another example is of a woman who meets a man that she likes, and thinking that the man is too handsome for her, she immediately creates resistance to manifesting love with him in her life. Thoughts like, "He is too handsome; he is too young; he is too rich; I am too dark; I am too fair; I am too short; I am too fat, etc." create solid doors of energy that prevent good from coming in. They are all self-defeating belief systems, which are just resistances.

When you experience lack of sunlight or fresh air in your home, you know that all you have to do is to pull back the curtains, and open the windows for sunlight and fresh air to come in, but what about the doors in your mind? Open them up, and let new, inspiring, and happy thoughts in. Just imagine what beliefs people carry with them, clouding their energy fields and creating resistance to good coming in?

Resistance happens because of beliefs that have set the mind into a particular mold. When the mind is in a mold, it finds it difficult to grow out of the mold and expand to include new possibilities, because it is not pliable enough nor trained enough to handle things easily, and so it resists. When the mind realizes that it has to expand, it experiences stress (manifestation stress), and this stress is the physical evidence of resistance.

> ### *This cycle can be broken when an inner change happens which helps the personality master the situation and consequently expand its universe.*

The minute you master something you are beyond it. What you have mastered is now within your portfolio of talents, and dealing with situations of the same nature now do not cause you stress, improving your attraction factor for good immediately. People listen to you, and what was once difficult for you becomes easy. Just don't create more stress for yourself in trying to master everything, or you can be caught up in this cycle also. Sometimes mere observation of a situation can release the situation for light to come in and heal it.

While resistance causes stress, you can reduce your resistance by relaxing your mind and body. As you relax, you allow in new energy of possibilities. Resistance can be physical or mental, and many times one can lead to another. Heal yourself of the resistance created by situations and belief systems. Some healing factors are: time, proper logic, self-empowerment, knowledge, love, physical workouts, nature and music; anything that is healthy and brings your attention to the now and cuts away from the negativity of situations, helps.

> ### *Energy is the building block of life and follows the path of least resistance.*

As long as a wall of fearful resistance exists, energy does not flow. Construct a dam across a flowing river and what happens? The water stops flowing. This is useful when you want water to collect, but not if you want it to flow freely. Water needs an opening to flow through. As you learn about energy and consciousness, you will also learn the skill of constructing thought dams that you can use to keep energy in, or to allow it to flow to where you want it to go. This ability to use energy constructively and masterfully comes from being more and more in the place of freewill.

An affirmation:

> ### *"It's attraction that draws things together and resistance that keeps them apart. I remove the reasons for resistance, so that what I want can come to me."*

5. FEAR

Most resistance happens because of fear. When you feel discomfort and fear toward a subject matter, you are not in alignment with the natural fulfillment of your desires.

What is fear?

+ A feeling of agitation and anxiety caused by the presence or imminence of danger.

+ A state or condition marked by this feeling; *living in fear.*

+ A feeling of disquiet or apprehension; *a fear of looking foolish.*

+ Extreme reverence or awe, as toward a supreme power.

+ A reason for dread or apprehension; *Being alone is my greatest fear.*

Fear prevents people from living life in a positive manner because it cripples from within, depriving a person of precious life energy and causing the entire system to curl up within itself, resulting in either fight or flight. When there is absence of fear, people think and act positively. Without fear each situation has a better chance to reach fruition.

Some fear is required in life, as in having respect for nature and treating people and situations with reverence and awe, and is also required to ensure survival. When you rid yourself of unnecessary fears, however, you actually open up energy, and what you want comes to you easily. Otherwise it is equivalent to erecting a ten-foot wall between you and what you want.

Fear keeps one bound and tied up, helpless to move freely in action, and creates a block to the feeling and expression of complete love and abundance. In true freedom, there is free expression of the love that you truly are.

When you dispense with unnecessary fear, you are able to spin wonderful dreams of success.

Remember that being free of unnecessary fear is not the same thing as foolish bravado. It is good to respect nature, just don't be bound by unnecessary fears.

An affirmation:

"I am taken care of by the universe and my Self. I am free of the fears that stop me from my happy goals."

As you connect more and more to your loving Self, you become convinced that your Self allows only good in, and this reduces fear. For example, as you believe that your loving Self will only take you into situations that are good for you, you will lose unnecessary fear and learn to relax.

6. BELIEFS

What you believe indicates the path that your mind will take in the creation of its stories. Depending on the stories that your mind spins, your thoughts send vibrations into the universe. So what do you believe?

+ Do you believe that you are sick and that conditions will never change?

+ Do you believe that there is no higher power, Higher Self, or God Self that will help you?

+ Do you believe that you are only a physical form at the mercy of nature's forces?

+ Do you believe that things are fated?

- Do you believe that someone does not love you?

- Do you believe that people are out to get you?

What do you believe?

It's not necessary to force yourself to believe things that are completely out of your range of thoughts right now, but if you allow for the tiniest seed of possibility to take root, it will grow into a truth and you will see that your changed beliefs go out like a wave to bring you matching responses.

We had discussed fear earlier. Just remember that fear is generated because of your beliefs. If you don't understand something and believe that something does not work well for you, you fear it.

Resistance, beliefs, and fear are all tied together. So first, work on your beliefs, release your fear, and remove the resistances that prevent Joyful Manifestation. When you believe that you can do something, that 'thing' is then within your area of easy skills and good flows to you easily.

If you believe, then things happen.

- You believe that you can easily buy a cup of coffee on your way to work, and so it happens. Affordability is not an issue here.

- You believe that you can walk to the bus stop, and so it happens. Physical limitation is not an issue here.

- You believe that you can breathe. Your system is perfectly capable of pulling in air and pushing it out, and it happens.

Yet, ask those who have a problem in these areas of life. Their beliefs do not allow them to afford a cup of coffee, walk a few steps, or even breathe comfortably. Question is, did the problems come up as a result of faulty belief systems, or did their belief systems become weak as a result of continuous exposure to problems, and pre-existing conditions? Whatever the reason, the Law of Attraction brings back more of what is already believed to be the truth. Nobody consciously invites problems into their lives. Buying a cup of coffee, walking, and breathing are very natural and normal for most people in the world, yet for some it is a problem, a huge mountain that needs scaling.

WHY IS THIS? IS IT KARMA?

It is karma to the extent that somewhere in the mind some emotional imprints exist from past lives and early childhood resulting in inability or acute difficulty in certain life areas that come easily for others. Certain vibrations relating to certain areas of life could be way off.

It is not wise to spend too much time finding out why and how the problems have come about, unless you can identify and then let go of the reasons for the fears. It is here, physically manifested, and bothering the current reality. That's all that matters. The question is how do you correct it? How do you make a mountain that is seemingly insurmountable into a tiny hill that you can easily climb? Maybe you can flatten it altogether.

By using creative thoughts, you can exercise your mental muscles so that your mind expands to allow for new possibilities. It may seem tough in the beginning, but just like a new marathon runner builds up his ability, little by little, and then in leaps and bounds until he feels that completing the marathon is an easy task, you too can build up your ability to do things that may seem to be beyond your capacity now. Once the mind expands to include possibilities, and once it can see itself climb that mountain, the body easily follows. Success happens! The energy vibrations are so pure and powerful at this point that you can actually land on the Moon (well, it's already been done. So let's choose some other heavenly place to land).

Believing that something is possible, releasing fears about it, and then allowing it to happen is the solution. In fact, there is no need to make it happen as it happens all by itself once the fear resistance blocking it dissolves. Divine forces awaken and takes you from point A to B, then to C, and all the way to Z. *Victory!*

An affirmation:

> *"I free myself of the fears that stop me from getting what I want. I change my beliefs when I know that they don't suit who I am. I believe only in good and that I can achieve my healthy and happy goals."*

7. DOUBT

Depending on what you believe, you may either feel self-confidence, or doubt. When you want to accomplish something, you should act from a place of confidence and not doubt. As long as doubt exists, it means that you don't completely believe in a positive outcome. Doubt can be in oneself, or in another. Doubt can take on any form and enter any situation. The minute that doubt enters the equation, things can start to go wrong.

Question: "Should I have blind faith?"

Faith is not blind as it is based on the very logical presumption of the working of a higher system or power, and when God is involved, it is okay to rest in his arms and take a deep breath of relaxation. After all, you don't worry about the Earth running off its course and colliding with other planets, do you? Don't you work on faith when you expect the Sun to rise every morning without fail? Do you doubt its intentions toward you and Earth? Do you doubt the stars and spend time wondering why they aren't shining during the day? You know that the stars are always there and shining. It is only you who cannot see them shine because the Sun is out during the day. Something was covering the shining stars—bright sunlight, and when the covering goes away at night, you will see the stars shine. Even the clouds that sometimes cover the stars are just temporary. Eventually they too drift away.

So when you don't doubt the universe and its functioning (at least I hope that you don't doubt it, and are not a believer in doomsday theories), why doubt the course of your life and every single thing in it? Why not trust that the person you like, likes you also? This again entails surrender. Everyone and everything are the arms and legs of the universe. The universe knows how to get the job done. Period. Doubt is a hindrance to Joyful Manifestation and can be reduced by surrendering it (the doubt) to the Divine.

In fact, you should doubt the negative and believe in the positive. Doubting the negative shakes its foundation and cuts the roots of the negativity taking hold in your life. So transfer your doubt to the negative, and keep faith in the positive. It changes your vibrations immediately.

An affirmation:

> ### "I trust in good and release all doubts into the universe for absorption and transmutation now."

8. NEGATIVE EGO

Though the human body is well suited for the gigantic feat of evolution, and God realization, it is also the most complicated and troublesome, as the human body comes with its unique friend and shadow, the human ego.

The ego is both a defense and offense mechanism, and even though not physically tangible like the human body, it can be felt every time you are uncomfortable about something. The ego is a part and parcel of the human personality and it is this personality which dictates how the ego works.

Ego can be positive or negative. If the ego feels good about itself, the ego works positively and allows you to be at ease in situations, but when it does not feel good, all hell can break loose. When a person feels negatively about himself and situations, he ceases to be at ease in situations, and the ego has a field day at the person's expense, not to mention everyone else who comes within its range. The actions taken by someone when his ego feels hurt depend how badly it is hurt. Some of the most violent actions taken by people around the world happen because of hurt caused to their ego, whether individually or collectively. The ego is fueled by emotions, and when the extent of hurt emotion is great, the ego rears its ugly head and actions are taken accordingly.

The negative ego is known to be the downfall of many. From the negative ego comes pride, greed, jealousy, doubt, anger, revenge, depression, lust, etc. The list is endless. This suitably imposes hurdles that slow down the process of final evolution on the spiritual, mental, and physical level.

An example of the damage that a negative ego can do is when a person feels so slighted because of his religious beliefs that he physically hurts others. He could even start a religious war. Of course, each situation has to be evaluated in itself, but if this person could just let go of his hurt and allow healing energy to flow in, he will find that the people who caused him hurt will be forced to change, or that he himself would find that there was nothing to be concerned about in the first place.

How does a positive ego help you?

If a person has a positive outlook about himself and toward life in general, less emotional hurt is stored, and when something out of the blue happens (for example, when a person is slighted) the person's ego is so well placed in the positive that this person simply shirks his shoulders and puts it down to a bad moment. No drama is required.

When you feel good about yourself, the need for negativity reduces and may cease altogether. Your attraction factor will then bring in the positive. Even if some zingers do come your way, you are able to easily sidestep them and move on, taking only such action as the situation requires, but from a space of light.

The ideal situation is for a person to have an ego that is flexible and self-healing. That is to say, if someone pushes you and causes hurt, you should be able to recognize the fact of the hurt and come back to your center by saying, "Yes I was hurt, but so what? I'm back and happier than ever." The stronger the push, the more time it may take you to come back to your center, but it should happen more quickly each time, and soon you won't feel pushed. Your ego will soon learn how to debug itself.

Though the human body enables you to accomplish evolution, it can also become a hurdle in the development of your consciousness. A fragile ego can play horrible tricks, putting your very happiness at risk. Because of this fragile ego, humans are quite capable of plotting destruction against one another, and against other creations.

An affirmation:

> *"The ego is my best friend and enemy. I use it skillfully to create good in my life and those of others. How I use my ego depends on me."*

9. LACK OF CONFIDENCE IN ABILITY

Closely connected to the negative aspect of the ego, lack of confidence can also play games with what you think you can do, who you think you are, and how beautiful or handsome you think you are. When you don't feel confident in your abilities, you experience fear and block good from flowing to you.

Lack of confidence is closely connected to your basic nature. People love to focus on their limitations. It is okay to be *aware* of your limitations and work on them to bring in positive change, but it is not good to *focus* on your limitations and to make them your truth. Lack of confidence is stored in your vibrations and sent out into the universe as a signal. You become the magnet and the target for every stray bullet, splinter, and stone. Hence you read about all the good guys who get targeted by bullies, and the good girls who are left behind with their hearts broken. It's because of weakness in their self-confidence.

As you become more confident about yourself, you attract good situations to you. Even if you are not actively enjoying your manifested dreams in the moment of now, with a bit of work you can be there, and if you can feel confident now, things will work out in your favor.

Be confident and content that everything is working out well, that the Divine has his fingers in the pie, and is monitoring everything. What a great space to be in, so confident and clear about positive outcomes.

An affirmation:

> *"I am good at everything I do.*
> *Everything I touch turns into gold."*

10. INABILITY TO STAY IN THE NOW

The now is what you really have, so dance away. The moment of now is everything and has power because it paves the way for all your future moments. You've heard these words spoken through the mouths of so many teachers, and some wonderful books have been written on this subject.

The mind is constantly involved in the past or the future. It is either thinking about what happened or will happen. It is either building dreams or complaining about things. It is rarely confident about the steps it takes, and keeps calculating profits and losses. Not only that, the nervous system generates a flood of emotions that further fuel these thoughts and gives them living color. It is essential that when you observe yourself caught up in the how and why of things that you come back to the present moment and break the thought circuit.

Being in the now means being okay in this current moment. Being okay now stills energy and allows for good energy to flow through. Every time you attach to a thought about the past or the future, you are robbing yourself of the now. It is in the now that you experience life and create all your future now moments. Using precious moments from the past to build the dreams of your future is okay, but this must be used skillfully without depriving yourself of your current moment. If you constantly live in the past or the future, it is as good as saying that your now is awful, and this is not a good energy to release into the universe.

Let's say that in your current moment of now you do have an issue that makes you feel bad. You don't have to cover your head and pretend beyond your abilities and make believe. If you can, in the moment of now, know that the current moment will pass, you will allow refreshing new energy in. Once you envision happiness coming in, your current moment of now will become perfect again. It stills and renews itself. For example, if someone is stuck in a bad apartment, he can imagine a new apartment where things are great. With this imagination he will feel so good that he allows happy energy in and his current moment of now becomes perfect. He is happy now. I know that it may seem as if he is still not in the moment of now since he is imagining something for the future, but it does help in bringing peace into the current moment, and that is what matters.

Don't be stuck in the future though, but bring in the future possibility of happiness into your now, for your enjoyment is in the moment of now.

Make your now precious and you will become a happy energy bundle. It's great to dream, but even while you are building your dreams, do so with an awareness of the now. Come back to the now, and take a deep breath in it. Remember that your current thoughts lead to more such thoughts, which create your reality. Relax, your now is perfect. *Smile!*

An affirmation:

"I am very much in the moment of now, and I love it. Life is perfect right now."

11. MISERY

What does misery feel like? Ask one who is miserable. Misery is a state of complete and total sadness. When one says that he is miserable it means that this person has gone beyond the state of just being sad. The energy of sadness has collected so much energy that it has now shifted into misery and taken over this person. To say "I am miserable" indicates complete despondency with the world, and this person's universe is not showing him even a facsimile of what he would like to see. This person's desires have been left unfulfilled so often that he experiences a constant feeling of being let down.

The word *misery* is connected to the word *miser*. The word miser describes one whose fists are closed so tightly that he does not give, either to himself or to others. He lives very meagerly in order to hoard money or whatever else that he thinks is or will be in short supply. Being a miser comes from the space of lack and not feeling provided for.

One who does not feel provided for, may not provide for others also. The universal flow stops in the hands of a miser. A miser does not see himself as a part of society and so does not think that he has to contribute to society by pouring in resources.

Being miserable is a state of being a miser with happiness. It happens when one does not allow the universe's healing energy to flow in or out. It is a state of great unhappiness which comes from pain, distress, ill health, lack, and feeling as if joy is absent in one's life along with the caring that the Divine normally provides. Here one closes oneself up to the Divine energies of caring and being taken care of. The energy field of one who is miserable is completely closed off to good energy coming through. If he does not allow good in, he does not spread happiness around either. Many people who are in the state of misery prefer to remain that way instead of allowing good to flow to and through them. Even when good knocks and seeks permission to enter, the one who is located in misery keeps all his doors and windows closed to good times and joy. There is so much distrust in the goodness of universal well-being that it seems almost impossible to one located in misery to be happy.

There is normally a trigger to get into the state of misery. In fact, many such triggers may exist. This trigger could be in the form of a situation or a cause that starts a ball of sadness to keep collecting more sadness until it becomes a huge ball of misery. Some common triggers are divorce, losing a loved one, loss of power, money, wealth, status, ill health, being in constant pain, being in war torn areas, family issues and failure in romantic love.

A miserable person does not allow the universal flow of happiness into his space at all. All walls are up and guarded, preventing good from coming in. Most people in misery walk with a closed and sometimes hunched over look rather than in an open manner. A person who remains in misery for a long time creates depression for himself, and for others. Unhappiness abounds, and the Sun stops shining in the life of one who is miserable.

A person who is miserable may start contemplating ways to get out of his misery, and these ways may be negative rather than positive. A person in extreme misery may even contemplate suicide as the end solution to getting out of his misery.

Why does continued misery make one think of suicide?

The mind can only take so much. It can only handle so much of not having hope until it caves in. A person who has a strong mind will not fall into misery in the first place, and will also find ways of getting out of his misery quickly. Someone who is unable to contemplate ways of getting out of misery in a happy manner may ultimately start thinking of ways that can end his misery permanently, that permanent solution being suicide.

The truth is that good is already inside you. Your joy is in you. If you feel that your joy is locked up in something outside of you, and because it is unavailable, you have to be miserable, then you are acting like the miser who locks up his money and does not allow even himself to enjoy it, because you are locking up your joy and not experiencing it.

Even though I speak of good knocking on the door and entering, it can happen in any way. Either someone can really come knocking, or good can be felt as a rush of happiness inside you first, and then someone comes knocking or calling. You must allow good into your life and get out of misery. Don't allow misery to build up anymore.

Remove this obstacle to Joyful Manifestation. Buy something nice for yourself, go dancing and do something that will reduce the feeling of being sad. Sadness is just a feeling and can be changed. You have the power to make positive changes in your life, dear one. You are very, very loved and are not alone. We all love you and are with you in this life journey.

An affirmation:

> *"I am happy. My heart is placed in joy.*
> *I am loved by all and the All now."*

Chapter Twenty–Two

~

Step 6: Get into the Correct Space

"Since I create from the space I am in, I always choose the space of well-being to live in, and to create from."

Even as you empower yourself, let go of negativity, and remove the obstacles to Joyful Manifestation, you become poised to move into the space of positive creation. The space of positive creation is where you will find the right energies to help you in your creation process. You will also find very useful co-creators in this more happy and healthy space.

You can deliberately navigate to the space that you would like to create from. By letting go, and clearing the obstacles that keep you from going forward, you get out of the space of continued negativity and conflict and get into a space in which you can fly freely and create. Think of yourself as a jet navigating away from land and cloudy skies, into clear skies, positioning yourself for a beautiful trip that will take you to the places you want to go.

Get into the space of positive creation and get ready for actual creation work. Let's look at how to navigate to this new space of active creation.

Every new state of being you attain creates a new attraction factor for you. Your consciousness contains imprints that dictate what happens to you. In order for your consciousness to contain new information and to attract new energy, it is good to clear it up and get into a new energy space. The following steps help get your mind into a new space where positive events can happen.

1. Realize the lesson

2. Be in the gap

3. Life layers and energy corridors—keep moving mentally from one level to another

1. REALIZE THE LESSON

Realizing the lesson gets you into a new layer of consciousness, and you emanate a different vibration that changes your attraction factor for the better.

If you have a problem, present the problem to your Inner Self and ask for another viewpoint. As your perspective changes, energy changes very quickly around you. Nobody can get you to hold onto a logic that you know does not serve you. All you have to do is to find a better feeling thought amongst the barrage of thoughts in your mind.

As your belief about something changes, so do your vibrations. Once you realize the lesson in a situation, everything starts to change immediately. This is because it is no longer necessary for you to be in a negative space, facing an unwanted reality.

People around you are like mirrors enabling you to see yourself in glorious splendor. If there is any characteristic in anyone or in any situation that bothers you, then look for it in yourself or look for the opposite of that trait. Ask for that characteristic to be changed in you or removed altogether if it is no longer of use.

For example, you could be the most loving person in the world, and yet have a tendency to argue your truth until you and everyone else turns blue in the face. When your soul recognizes that it no longer wants this trait and wants to release it forever, it will create situations that allow for you to first recognize it, then release it and create lasting and permanent change in your personality. When you release a characteristic that no longer serves you, your vibrations change and you stop attracting situations where you are forced to defend yourself in arguments, and worse still in anger or physical violence. The need for defensive behavior reduces dramatically.

If you have the opposite problem of not speaking your truth and holding things within yourself, you can change this too for the better. You may recognize this trait when you encounter situations that make you come face to face with it. Maturing is also part of being a Master Manifester. As you develop positive and powerful qualities in you, the universe gives you bigger and better things to be responsible for. The universe will never give you things to take care of unless you are prepared for it. As you blossom into the flower that you were always meant to be, you will attract wonderful situations of amazing well-being.

For example, inculcating the qualities of commitment allows you to attract more clients in your business as this quality is beeped out into the universe, attracting wonderful attention toward you. People all over the world want to give you their business as they recognize that you will deliver.

Realizing the lesson changes your vibration immediately. As you change your inner world by realizing things, you start to feel joyful inside, uncomplicated by life's difficulties. You start to be a joy machine that keeps churning out good vibes all the time. As your inner psychological world changes, your outer world also changes. Realizations take you into a new space that is better suited for joyful creation. Having realizations is not about something being wrong with you. It is about realizing your beauty, your efficiency, your true commitment to this world, to yourself, to your family, your positive outlook in life, your joy, the love that this universe holds for you, etc. The list is endless. Each realization positions you to be a better creator. Each realization takes you closer to your true light. Having realizations about situations takes you one step closer to your goal. For example, when you realize that someone really likes you, you are many steps closer to your goal of manifestation. In fact, you are there! You can get your realizations from statements made, actions taken, subtle inferences, not so subtle inferences, etc.

The realization process is very effective to change your attraction point. Be the change that you want to see happen. Recognize and let go of unwanted traits and characteristics, and inculcate those qualities which enable you to be happy and successful in life. Let go of the negatives, and set the foundation to be established in abundance.

2. BE IN THE GAP

What does it mean to be in the gap? Let's find out.

The in-built survival mechanism of any living organism is to respond or react to dangers and provocations in a way that best protects the mental and physical safety of the organism. This mechanism is required for the preservation and perpetuation of life. As a species' nervous system gets more evolved, its emotional range also evolves along with its responses. It can stop, think, and then act. Even for humans who are supposed to be the most evolved of living creatures on this planet, the response system to dangers can sometimes be extreme. In fact, many people around the world who live lives of violence or hatred have response systems that fall within the victim-attack bracket. The more victimized a person feels, the more fight or flight response is imprinted into his psyche. Negative fight or flight responses can sometimes be so severe that it could be detrimental to a person's safety and that of society itself.

There is a gap that needs to be introduced between provocation and action. Any action taken from the space of provocation is not an original action, but is a reaction. Such a reaction will end up having consequences, and so it is best to develop the habit of pausing between an event and your response to the event. This is the gap that needs to be introduced before an event and an action, allowing your thoughts to change and result in mature action.

For example, if Kimberly hurts your feelings, what happens? Hurt thoughts containing hurt energy come up and a mood sets in (anger or sadness) and you may either attack her verbally, or withdraw from her.

When you introduce the ability to pause between an event (the provocation) and an action, your thoughts then have the chance to cool down and reform themselves into something that will be useful to you when you do act. When you are in the gap, energies still around you, giving you time to connect to Source and act from this space. When you are in the gap you are open to Source's loving guidance. If you act from the space of provocation, you will create situations that resonate with the vibration of the provocation, but when you connect to Source, you feel more self-love and will consequently act from this elevated place and have wonderful experiences.

+ A person who has self-love has confidence and does not react to provocations to his detriment.

+ A person who has self-love reduces the number, and severity of provocations that come his way.

+ A person who has self-love feels connected with society at large, does not feel the need to cause harm to anyone, and in fact turns his attention toward helping others.

When you start to feel self-love, you will be able to stop, think, and act skillfully. The feeling of self-love increases as you are able to introduce more gaps between your thoughts. When you focus on the gap between two thoughts, you connect to Source, and rest in your true nature of peace. In the gap, nothing happens. Literally; there is nothing. When you connect to this nothingness, you can create anything.

Your nervous system rests in the gap, and energy stills around you. You release stress and karmic imprints that would have otherwise added to the amount of emotion that you feel when provoked. When there is less emotion behind your actions, you can act with skill. Even if you must speak in anger because a situation requires it, you will be able to do it without stress. Practice being in the gap more and more; it is a place of true rest.

3. LIFE LAYERS AND ENERGY CORRIDORS— KEEP MOVING MENTALLY FROM ONE LEVEL TO ANOTHER

At any given time you are in a particular layer of energy, and you get to experience the reality contained in that layer. For example, when airplanes fly, each airplane flies at a certain height and has its own flying space and experiences the weather that exists at that height. To escape any turbulence (which may exist at the level of the clouds, for example) it has to climb up to higher levels so that it may now comfortably cruise at the selected level of say 33,000 feet. It then travels in this air corridor safely and smoothly.

If you feel that you are living in energy that is not conducive to your success and happiness, after learning whatever has to be learnt in that energy, ascend and start flying in clear skies. Don't get caught up in the seeming reality of the problems prevalent in the lower airspace. You need to be in a happy space in order to create good situations. Climb up to the space that you would love to create from and position yourself for creation. All thoughts come according to the space you are in, and these thoughts also help keep you in that space. So if you feel that your thoughts are reflective of an unhealthy space, change them.

Just because you are witnessing a particular reality does not mean that you have to be stuck in it. Once you know that you can change your life just by changing your consciousness, you won't get stressed from thinking that nothing changes, and will know that you can usher in new energies of hope and positive expectations whenever you want. Even though you may not like what is going on currently in your life, as you change your consciousness and take guided action from this new mental space, you will witness a reality closer and closer to what you really want. Your conscious mind along with your body, are the tools that your soul uses to experience the physical world. If you don't like a particular reality, then just ask for a change. Ask your Inner Self to create a new reality for you, and in the meantime, do work on your resistances and remove your blocks to good coming in. As your Self makes these changes, your karmic energy changes and affects the behavior of the external world toward you, since your energy envelopes and infiltrates everyone.

Self-empowerment, letting go, removing obstacles, and having realizations help change energy. Music and other self-help methods are also wonderful ways to change energy. Anytime you feel like you are being drawn into lower energy, get into a positive space so that you can attract good situations to you.

Chapter Twenty-Three

~

Step 7: Create the Situation

"I create joyfully."

It is difficult to create good from a space that is cloudy and contains hurt energy. Now that you have moved into a better space, you should feel better. You can verify the fact of feeling better if you are able to breathe in cool, soothing air (even if you live in a warm climate, you will feel as if you can breathe easily), your heart feels free and open, and you have easy access to a smile. If you are able to say, "Woo hoo," and feel active joy course through you, know that you are well placed for wonderful creation.

Normally in this space, good gets drawn to you like a magnet all by itself. You can get specific about what you'd like to experience, so get your manifestation gloves on and let's create. The creation process includes asking, but at this stage it is more about intending, affirming, and asking from feeling good rather than asking from contrast. Simply follow the steps given below:

1. Feel good

2. State your intention

3. Create a dominant vibration

4. Visualize

5. Maintain high expectations

6. Affirm the happening, and thank the universe

1. FEEL GOOD

Asking from the contrast is the opposite of gratefulness and appreciation, which is the space of feeling that you already have something and are thankful for it. You appreciate its presence in your life because you are actively enjoying it. If you can somehow manage to get into the space of gratefulness and appreciation, even while not actually having in hand what you want, it will help. When gratitude happens, the vibrations of gratitude reach out and ring bells in the universe, opening the doors of heaven wide to let good in, because in that moment of gratitude you feel as if you already have what you want. In fact, even a tiny moment of gratitude is enough to open up the universal doors for you. In that moment, wonderful healing happens, love abounds, and everything is well.

Well-being is the natural order of things and it peaks in moments of deep gratitude and appreciation.

In the space of wellbeing, it feels as if everything is okay with the world and things are just right. The now moment is so special that all other previous moments of anger and sadness are suspended and lose connection with this moment of extreme perfection. It is the space of grace.

Just as you can ask for what you want by observing what you don't want, you can also ask for what you want by feeling good with what already is, is in the process of becoming, or what you feel it could become. For example, let's say that you want to be slim, and you ask for a great figure by observing the contrast of being overweight. While losing weight, you could start to feel good about the fact of losing weight and looking slimmer (even marginally slimmer), which creates good vibrations and attracts what you want even more quickly.

It is not always necessary to create only from observing the contrast as a negative. You can also shoot out an asking and consciously create from good feelings. For example, feeling good about your developing business really starts to put you into alignment with what you really want to see happen—that your business would be more profitable.

So how can you feel good about things?

Do you have a memory of some good moments? For example, do you have a memory of having money in your bank account even though currently you may not have much? Well, access those memories and feel good about them. As you recall moments of perfect well-being and happiness about situations, you will shoot out good-feeling vibes into the universe, pulling forth reasons to feel even better.

So what happens when you feel good?

When you feel good, your mind relaxes, good thoughts surround you, and your heart opens up for speedy manifestation. Your heart needs to feel secure. You need to feel secure, and when you feel secure, your resistance comes down and you open up to good news. Until you start feeling good about situations, your heart has its door closed and you feel resistance. This resistance blocks the manifestation of what you really want. Start to feel good about things, feel your heart open up, and allow good into your life.

Remember that everything is a part of nature, and nature is a part of God. God is present in nature everywhere. This is why many cultures worship nature as God because God is nature itself. You are a part of nature. What you want to see happen is also subject to nature. When you get empowered in a happy way, you will attract to you amazing situations that align with what you really want. What you don't want to see happen reduces and dwindles away into nothingness.

Healing happens when nature is as aligned with your well-being as you are with hers. Invoke nature to help you with your life areas, and she will control her various elements and have them working well for you. Celebrate Mother Nature as your loved one and she will celebrate you. Enjoy all of her various wonders; the seas, the wind, the Sun, the skies, the rain, the trees, plants, mountains, life forms; simply celebrate her and her amazing beauty. Help her take care of her creations, as she is a concerned mother who cares about everything that lives in her, on her, and around her. Feel good about her.

Feeling good is like a thank you note to the universe for all that has been given, received, is already in use, and will continue to be in joyful use.

2. STATE YOUR INTENTION

State your intention. What would you like to see happen? An intention is a declaration of what you want to see happen and it carries the power of your will behind it. When you make an intention, your energy field gears up because your consciousness comes together to see something through to manifestation. As soon as you intend something, changes happen in your thinking and your mind starts to prepare itself for that intention to be fulfilled by taking required action.

Sometimes when people get really tired of situations and they figuratively hit the wall, they can create intentions that will help them navigate out of these situations. For example, when someone gets really tired of his job, he might make an intention that is so severe that all actions that he takes from that point on work toward getting him out of the job. Please don't follow this as my advice, but as something that you must know so that you keep an eye on your intentions and the possible repercussions. You should not be surprised by what happens when an intention is made and forces align to make the intention happen. Actions are taken, yours or someone else's that may completely surprise you as all forces gather together to get you out of that situation.

A sample intention:

"I intend to marry so and so."

I know that several people would caution you against specifying a name or putting a face to it, but there is no harm. You will realize when you are getting overly attached to the name and face to your detriment, and will know how to let go. If you do not want to put a name and face to what you intend, you could say:

"I intend to marry someone who will keep me happy."

People use intentions when they feel empowered to declare what they want to create. They know that their will carries weight in this universe, and the heavens would realign just to make their intentions manifest into reality. When you state your intention, your consciousness gears up to create what you want. As your consciousness gears up, the universe starts to reflect this change, and a set of coincidences happen that enable you to get what you want. That which is the best match to your requirements will start to reveal itself for you to choose from and you will see a chain appear for you to grasp and reach where you need to be and so knowing your intention is very important.

The power of your intention, when used for common good, brings good back to you. There are many powerful intenders in this world who have intended harm against certain people, countries, etc. They don't live happy lives, and they spend their time hiding from the armed forces of various countries in mountains and deserts. What is the point of such intentions? Be a happy intender who intends good for himself and the world. Everyone and everything in this world belongs to you, and they look to your happy and peaceful intentions for their well-being and safety. Intend good for nature and her creations, and you will be welcome and very well protected everywhere. A happy intender is powerful, as he knows that what he intends will happen and is already happening.

Using intentions should come from a space of clarity after letting go of the issues, fears, and limitations that may have kept you bound up till now. If you find that you are still holding onto past negativity, then practice clearing the conflicts in your mind again. There is no harm in going back to a previous step in the ten-step Joyful Manifestation process, and then get back to this step again.

Intentions come from a space of self-empowerment where your words have value and are done because you said so.

3. CREATE A DOMINANT VIBRATION

After getting into a good energy space where you can breathe freely, feel good, and state your intention(s), catch onto one strong positive in the whole situation and make it your dominant vibration. For example, if someone that you know keeps losing his job, anchor to the idea of the person being so capable that he would easily attract a new job that matches his abilities. Hold onto the positive indications you get, and come out of all the other weakening elements of the situation which are playing around, reducing the strength of the positive vibrations, like a poor economy, etc.

Focus on the positive points in any situation, because what you focus on expands to create your reality. Your mind is like a car and can travel in any direction. You are the driver who can intend it to go in the direction of your choice. In the same way, your mind is also like a hand that can catch and pull on any rope, bringing in a flood of whatever that rope is attached to. In any situation, take the time to halt and see the many ropes hanging within your reach. These ropes indicate your choice of thoughts about a situation. Pull on whatever you want to see happen, and not on what you don't want.

Learn how to focus selectively on what you want. This may be hard to do in the beginning, but once you know how to do this, you will soon align with what you want to see happen, instead of exposing yourself to all the stones, pieces of glass, and other sharp objects and garbage that may be thrown at you. Learn to focus until you see what you want to see; keep on adjusting and fine tuning until what you want to see comes fully into your vision.

When you think a thought a few times and put emotion behind it, you start to create your dominant vibration. You may even find yourself affirming the thought and making it your truth. For example, if a family member succeeds in getting you to react in a certain way a few times, very soon you may find that it becomes your truth as you affirm: "She's always this way. She always makes me feel like this." It becomes your reality and you may start the process of unmanifesting the person from your life, and unless you find some other good-feeling thoughts that you can give power to, it can become your destiny. You can improve the situation by thinking: "But she's so sweet and treats me well most of the time," and so on until you create a dominant vibration about being treated really well by this person, which then becomes your truth. What you make into your reality is up to you.

Sometimes the balance may be so fine that while this person is nice, she can still get you to feel badly about yourself. Both sides being equal in weight, you may have a really hard time trying to latch onto the positive in the situation and making it your dominant vibration. If you really want something and feel that there is hope, keep changing your perspective of the situation, even if just a bit at a time. Whenever you see a situation as having faults in it, try to remove this feeling of the situation being flawed. See someone that you think is sick as already healed and well, because the truth is that he is not sick. Adopting a 'no flaws' approach to difficult situations may be hard, but you will become good at it with practice. When you create a positive dominant vibration, you will see your dreams come true, which brings us to the next step—seeing.

4. VISUALIZE

The sweet dreams of your life are visions sent up by your Self, who is the actual seer. Visions are sent up by this seer who experiences life from within you. Visualization is a happy process where visions come floating up by themselves, and the feelings that you have when these visions come up are good.

Sometimes these happy visions are easy to see, and sometimes it is the hardest thing ever. When forces seem to gather against manifestation, getting your mind's eye to see what you want to see happen, can be hard, and I am making an understatement here. When sweet moments happen however, visions of the beautiful future you want to create come floating up from within you like a dream. This normally happens when the mind is still and you are not troubled by any issue, either past or current, which is why it is important to be in a good space for useful visualization.

When your mind gets troubled by happenings, these visions get blocked. The mind is like a vessel for the sweet dreams of the Self, which is constantly creating its life. When your mind gets troubled with issues, the vessel is already full of turmoil and cannot receive these sweet visions. However, if your mind is clear and these sweet visions can come up, they create a dominant vibration for you to attract good. Sometimes the attraction factor is so great that when these visions come up physical manifestation happens quickly, even before your mind registers what is happening. In fact, most things that happen naturally for you do so because of what the Self has seen for itself. It just happens so fast that you, the personality, do not even have the time to make a connection between the vision and the happening. The trick is to keep your mind free of trouble and allow your Self, the true Creator, to send up happy visions for manifestation.

The clearer your mind, the faster and better your manifestations.

Just think of the ocean. When the ocean is still, you can see the bottom at places. The same logic applies to your Self. When your mind is still, you can see the seer working for you, spinning your life's contents in joy.

Visualization and imagination

Happy visualization is not a forced thing. It has to come from the space of joy, which is your True Self. It comes when the mind is free of stress. Relaxing your mind allows the Self's sweet visions to come up and manifest themselves. Imagination is a process of the mind, which is different from the original sweet visions of the Self. Positive imagination is also good, because if you can get your mind to imagine happy situations, you change your vibrations for the better. I don't have to teach you how to imagine, but here is how you can deliberately work with your Self to send up good visions. Take a few minutes for yourself and follow the steps given below:

a. Sit in a comfortable position, preferably with your hands in an open position on your knees, indicating receptivity.

b. Take a few deep breaths, and feel yourself relax.

c. Ask your Divine Self to send you good manifesting thoughts and visions on the desired subject.

d. Allow thoughts to come up and play around, but don't attach to any one thought. Many of these thoughts may be blocks to manifestation just coming up for clearing. Let them come up. Watch them as if they were passing clouds. When resistance comes up as thoughts, it gets cleared away.

e. You will start to feel as if you are free and happy, softer and lighter.

f. Good thoughts about the subject matter in question will now start to come up.

g. Allow your good feelings to respond to these positive thoughts, and feel happy.

h. If in the first attempt with the process you feel happy, but not happy enough, go as far as you can with this process and repeat it with breaks in between until you feel really good about the situation.

i. The visions should make you feel really good about what you are asking for. As you receive these visions, get ready for good news.

Let go of all stress, and make your mind empty of negativity so that Joyful Manifestation happens easily for you. The idea is not to fear all negativity, but to become a skilled manifester who knows what works and what does not work.

5. MAINTAIN HIGH EXPECTATIONS

Some teachers advocate dropping all expectations, and there is a reason behind this. Having no expectations is another form of letting go. As long as partial expectations exist with a good dose of expecting bad, then you are swimming upstream. Releasing all expectations allows you to feel good and to just float.

There are people who struggle with making a relationship work and lose all their energy in it. In such situations it better to stop having any immediate expectations from the relationship, which allows you to rest and decide what you want to do, whether it is to open up for new and better relationships, or for the old one changing into a better form which can happen once calm energies move in. Having no expectations is optimal for attaining a state of peace in a situation where you have no say because of where it is situated in your mind. If something is not well situated in your mind, it is best to drop all expectations, surrender, and fly in the arms of the Divine.

Having high expectations is where you fully expect good to come to you. Even when you drop all expectations for a particular outcome, you can still expect general good as there is nothing that stops you from expecting good under all circumstances. It's your choice to be someone who expects only good to happen. "What the mind can conceive, the eyes can see." I have found that the sooner people start to shift their expectations, the better for their reality, which changes in response to each such shift.

> ### *Your expectations regarding what you want determine the road that you take, and your destiny.*

If your expectation of a situation is negative, then you end up swimming upstream, but if you have positive expectations, then your attraction factor is good and you flow toward positive outcomes easily. As you make even subtle shifts in your thinking, your path and destiny change accordingly. In fact, your path and destiny depend upon your expectations of situations. For example, if you expect your favorite restaurant to serve you the best pasta, you will take the effort required to get there, won't you? If you don't expect to be served good food, however, then you may choose not to travel the distance required. When you feel confident about a situation, it increases your attraction factor to get what you want.

What should you do if you are not able to maintain the correct level of expectation required? For those cases where you find it difficult to retain your joyful expectations, surrender helps. Surrender to the Divine power. Not everything has to be worked out by you. You may just end up having a delightful surprise waiting for you. The trick is in giving up the worry in a situation and seeing it unravel beautifully in front of you. State what you'd like to see happen clearly, and then let go. Meanwhile, work on having positive expectations and increase your confidence. Remove all resistance that reduces your expectations. This is not about expecting from a feverish and attached point of view, but expecting from the space of knowing that something is already yours. It really tilts things in your favor, and the universe will make a way for you. Keep seeing good visions and create good energy for the future you want to see happen.

6. AFFIRM THE HAPPENING, AND THANK THE UNIVERSE

Affirmations are widely recommended today as a way of shifting people from negative thinking into positive thinking. A common problem that people have is in thinking, "I have been making affirmations for years now, yet nothing much has changed."

How do affirmations help, and what is the correct way to use affirmations?

Making affirmations is equivalent to issuing commands to your energy system. It has the effect of changing the vibration of your energy so that the Law of Attraction can bring back matching experiences.

Saying an affirmation starts a process where the power contained in that affirmation reaches out and starts making energy changes. It is a declaration from that person to start bringing in the energy vibrations contained in the affirmation into his life. Even though the person making the affirmation wants what he is affirming to start happening in his life, an affirmation is always made from the space that *it is already happening*. As a person starts affirming, the effect is slow until he starts to feel the truth behind the affirmation. When a person feels the truth of the affirmation, the affirmation gathers strength and powerfully changes the person's energy field to bring in positive results.

The affirmation process, when accompanied by a process of realization, increases its power tenfold. When a person goes "Aha", and experiences a shift in thinking, his whole energy field shifts to allow new energy to come in, and the Law of Attraction responds accordingly.

Making affirmations without feeling the impact of the words is like applying a band-aid to an internal problem. The issue remains within while disinfectant and ointment is applied outside. Why is this?

It's because there is a whole well of negativity within, and applying some positive medicine on the outside is like surface cleaning. What really has power is the well of negativity within over the light application of positive affirmations.

For example, if a woman affirms "I am beautiful," and she says this over and over again, yet she does not really feel beautiful or have an "aha" moment where she is struck by how truly wonderful she is, the affirmations have little effect. If a man keeps affirming "I am rich and getting richer every minute," but his eye is on his bank balance and he feels bad about spending money, the affirmations have little to no effect. If, however, the man has a moment of realization where he feels that he is blessed because all his expenses are met and he is taken care of, he feels so rich that his affirmations take hold immediately. When an affirmation takes hold and gets embedded in a person's energy field, then thoughts of beauty, well-being, and abundance keep drifting up into the consciousness all by themselves, creating many wonderful moments to savor.

Affirmations are very powerful, for they come from the space that you already have what you asked for and you affirm its presence in your life. Feeling beautiful, rich and healthy in the moment of now allows your affirmations to work wonderfully. Affirmations come from the belief that what you want to see happen will happen and is already happening. It is not from the space of hoping against hope or asking futilely, but is from the space of seeing what you intend as already happening. If you have prayed for it, cleared energies, and have visualized somebody calling you, then it is time for an affirmative way of thinking. He or she will call you, and that's that.

You can affirm the fact of receiving the call and thank the universe for it.

To understand this better, think of someone handing you a cashier's check. The check is in your hands, and all you have to do is to make a deposit and have the money flow into your bank account. You have asked, cleared energies, gotten yourself into a good space mentally, intended, visualized, and are now affirming the receipt of what you want and are saying "thank you" in advance. Know that your affirmations have power in this stage of the Joyful Manifestation process. Just know it.

An example of a thankful affirmation is:

"I thank the universe for Sam's call. His call made me feel really good."

Sam has not actually called yet, but your thank you note has already gone out for his call, a call that made you feel good. You have asked, cleared, situated yourself, intended, visualized, and have affirmed the receipt with a thank you to the universe. Can you feel the power of affirmations now?

Chapter Twenty–Four

~

Step 8: Take Skillful Action

"Correctly situated, I take skillful action."

After having an image of what you want, creating a dominant point of attraction, and expecting good, be prepared for the next step—action. The space you are in creates action, which brings back consequences. Here action includes inaction, because not acting when required has its own consequences.

Action does not stop. It continues with some rest in between. The need to act may arise on many occasions, and most times this action happens because of the need to respond either to an external happening, an inner urge, or a combination of the two. Many times the inner urge happens because of an external event.

Even though in the spiritual realm, it is the vibration of the Being that counts, when this Being takes on a physical body, action becomes part of the parcel. Brought down to physicality, mental experiences translate into physical ones.

> *What you experience in your mind can happen in the physical so if you want to take correct action, think correctly.*

The space you are in matters, since this mental space will dictate your physical actions. A good example is of a businessman who thinks that he is unable to make profits. This mental space of non-profitability will translate into the physical action of closing down his business, and that is such a loss to him and society. If he could, with some skilled action prompted by a good mental space, take correct steps, he could turn around his business, make a lot of money, and also provide a valuable service to society.

Since consequences are connected to action, let's discuss what comprises skillful action. The ability to take skillful action depends upon certain factors:

1. Ability to comprehend truth

2. Attachment to situations

3. Healing of hurt and feeling free

4. Intention behind manifestation

5. Ability to choose wisely

6. Strength of conviction

7. Ability to be centered

8. Ability to respond efficiently

1. ABILITY TO COMPREHEND TRUTH

As something starts to slip into your awareness, it starts to become your truth. It takes on a life of its own as if a separate entity, and motivates your intentions and actions. It has its own power of attraction as it vibrates in your energy field, causing the Law of Attraction to bring you evidence of the truth, further establishing it into your consciousness and that of the universe. After all, your consciousness pervades the universe, doesn't it?

Awareness creates and fuels truth. As you change your awareness, you change your truth.

Yes, as you change your awareness (in general and with regard to individual situations) you can change your truth. Truth is subjective. It completely depends on the situation, varies from case to case, and may even vary from minute to minute. The same yardstick cannot be used in all situations. What is required is a sense of intuition to be able to see beyond the surface at the underlying truth. The same situation can mean different things to different people. The same words can change meaning depending on the eyes reading the words. As you attempt to understand the truth behind a situation, know that the truth is what **you choose** to see as real.

Truth is one and manifold at the same time.

If you read some of the teachings on parallel dimensions and the like, you will see that for every situation there are many possibilities that co-exist together in energy, just waiting for you to focus on, and make one your truth.

What you make your truth will decide your action. When you decide your ultimate goal, you can also decide to choose your truth carefully. Be able to see the long chain of actions and reactions that can result from adopting something as your truth in this moment of now, knowing that truth can change depending on what you pay attention to. Choose carefully to adopt as your truth that which will serve you best.

What you choose to see as truth will guide your thoughts and actions. For example, if Nancy notices that her boyfriend John is acting strange, she can do one of the following:

1. She can start to suspect that John is cheating on her, start to build on that as the truth in her mind, investigate the issue, and end up proving herself right, or

2. She can let go, work on her inner feelings, ask for a wonderful solution, and choose to see something else as her truth. If she can successfully focus on what she would like to see as the truth (John as a loving and devoted man) she can avert a possible issue, and change the course of her life unless ofcourse the truth has built up really huge and cannot be changed in time.

Even as Nancy adopts an approach that suits her, perceiving truth as she would like to see it, she must also work on her confidence and know that she is so amazing that John would never dream of cheating on her. This of course takes one back to self-empowerment and self-realization. It's okay to go back to a previous step, strengthen your vibrations and come back to this one to perceive things differently. Now what she perceives can be the Universal truth also, because her mind pervades everything and everyone.

So many people around the world have adopted so many ideas, made them into a truth, and spent time spinning stories. The next thing they know, their so-called truth is now bigger than them—bigger than everything, and it becomes a huge monster that is difficult to tackle. All actions now have to be taken according to this huge truth, and many of the actions may not be pretty at all. This is the reason that war happens; this is the reason that people spend lifetimes running, hiding, and hurting other people.

A key to skillful action is to adopt truths that will give rise to action and results that you would like to see happen. Feel out your truth and sense if it gives rise to more love or more hatred. Your nervous system will let you know.

The nature of the action you take depends on what you think is the truth of a situation.

2. ATTACHMENT TO SITUATIONS

I call this adverse attachment to situations, people, and things. Ultimately, we are human and so the tendency to love and get attached does exist. A lot of people perceive attachment as something really bad, but it needs to be understood in the correct context. Love energy is good; in fact, it is great. Needy and adverse love energy however is unhealthy, because needy love can turn into anger and hatred at any moment. All it requires is a trigger. That's all.

The reason that attachment is not advocated is because when attachment happens and you are not able to get what you are attached to, disappointment sets in. After a while, this continued disappointment turns into resentment and anger, which then dictates your actions. Anger-tinged action can destroy families, societies, and countries. So rid yourself of the adverse attachment to things, people, places, thoughts, and beliefs, and allow yourself to act from a space of freedom. Of course, only you can decide what you want to give importance to and what you don't want to give importance to. Like I mentioned before, truth varies from person to person and from situation to situation.

When action happens from a space of light love, the action promotes more love and happiness. If action happens from the space of fearful and adverse attachment, the action is mostly confused and hurtful.

Let's look into this further. There are four main types of wealth that people love to attain and then spend time preserving:

1. Money and property

2. Love through relationships

3. Power

4. Reputation

Think about it. Most of your time may be spent in pursuing one or all of the above, because there is an idea that happiness is attached to it. Whichever is your source of joy, don't worry; there is no need to feel guilty about wanting things and making ways to get those things into your life, but it is important to practice one principle in its acquisition and its maintenance— love without adverse attachment. It can mean all the difference between being happy and being unhappy.

Let's say that you saved up and bought the car that you always wanted. What happens when you drive that car or even see it parked in your drive way? Do you enjoy it? Do you feel happy? Great! You bought it because the thought of owning and driving the car created a sense of pleasure in you, and now it's yours to enjoy.

But what happens if your car gets scratched? Do you feel sad and upset? Some emotion is expected of course (we are human), but how you handle the incident and turn it around will contribute to making or breaking your attraction for continued fortune or misfortune.

A wonderful yard stick is asking:

Will this thought and consequent emotions increase my fortune or misfortune?

If you don't get upset at all, then hats off to you!

If you do get upset, but you are able to get around the initial upset with new thoughts like, "It doesn't matter. It can be fixed", "Next time I'll be more careful", "I'll ask the angels to take care of it", etc., then you are doing well. You will continue to enjoy your car with the same love that you had for it earlier, and your good fortune vibrations will pick up again and continue to be steady.

If, however, you allow your sadness to continue, and you feel angry, despondent, vengeful, as if this always happens to you because the world is out to get you, then it means that you are attached to your car in a negative manner. Your sense of confidence to bounce back is not strong enough to weather the negative happening, and anything that happened to the car reflects on your life. The one event of your car connects to other negative events, and what is called forth is a huge tide of unhappiness.

Ultimately, this has nothing to do with the car, but has a lot to do with your sense of well-being. If you have a strong of sense of well-being, then such events will not create turbulence, and you can even turn them around to your advantage. "Thank God that it is only a scratch on the car and nobody was hurt. Thank you, thank you, thank you universe." What a wonderful turnaround!

Okay, now your question is: What if something even worse than a scratch happens to your car? We will discuss this in the next point on healing hurt, as it is better addressed there, but for now just know that adverse attachment attracts the possibility of hurt.

Don't be attached to anything to your own detriment.

This has nothing to do with loving something or enjoying it, but your sense of enjoyment must not be upset by damage or loss to your possessions, because your ability to rebound and get back quickly into good fortune vibes really depends on it.

If you carry adverse attachment energy for anything in your life, be it land, house, people, reputation and/or power, know that it will become a weakness for you, which means that whatever you are attached to may attract hurt. Your personal happiness must not depend upon external factors. Instead, know that it is because you are happy within that you have and will continue to attract and maintain good.

Let's look at this more closely. Why are you attached to something? It's because at some level you don't believe that it is yours, or that it will continue to be there for your enjoyment. A Master Manifester knows that what he wants is already his and will always be there for his enjoyment. He need not be adversely attached to it and can feel free until it comes into his physical presence for actual enjoyment. Attachment indicates a string used to tie something to you, like the pens in banks are tied to counters. The pens are tied because the chances of people walking away with them, either forgetfully or deliberately are very high. Do you really want to live your life being adversely attached to things and people? Ask yourself:

"Do I really want to tie this thing or person to me out of the fear of losing it/him?"

Attachment from the space of fear is adverse attachment.

At the same time, you don't have to be detached from things in order to avoid attachment.

Being detached means taking deliberate effort not to care about people and things because you are scared of getting attached or hurt and is not a very good place to be either. It may be acceptable in the beginning stages to practice deliberate detachment just to overcome negative attachment, but not indefinitely. There is no need to push away people and things from you and it is okay to love and to be loved. It is okay to enjoy money and all of its benefits. You do not have to be detached from all of this just to prove that you are not attached. If you are detached, then know that you are not truly enjoying whatever the Divine brings you, which means that it may become redundant and the universe may even stop giving you opportunities to have those very things.

Just like attachment makes you tie something to you because you fear losing it, detachment might make you take up a sword and cut all ties, and this detachment comes from the fear of losing the very thing that you love. It is okay to distance yourself for some time while you are discovering your true self-worth, but not because you are afraid of attachment. A much better way is to practice love and passion without adverse attachment. This allows you to enjoy your life and whatever you have in it without fearing loss because if you are attached, you cannot really enjoy something because of all the fear that surrounds it.

It is great to be free, knowing that everything is okay and is in divine and perfect order. In this space you can truly enjoy life. *Love attracts people to you, but it has to be joyful love and not fear-filled.* When you are not adversely attached to anything, you experience a wonderful feeling of freedom, which lays the foundation for skillful action.

Action that is free of needy attachment, but taken with love, is good action.

3. HEALING OF HURT AND FEELING FREE

Good action comes from a healthy mental space.

Let's be practical. These are real people and real lives we are talking about here. People are loaded with all sorts of worries and have all sorts of attraction points. People attract all kinds of things to them, and they are busy resolving issues, back tracking, undoing what they have done, and recovering from the rebound effects of their actions.

Hurt created from the past tends to be stored in the memory, and future actions are then based on that hurt. Many times you may not even have the time to stop and think. You see a person, connect to a strong and sad feeling, vent it out, and act accordingly. This can and does happen all the time in this world. Maybe what you love was hurt by another. It could be that a job was lost, or someone was insulted or injured. It is enough to get anyone really upset, and you cannot then say, "I am detached." Feelings do get hurt and emotions do rise up. You are after all human.

Here is what you can do in such situations:

1. First, acknowledge that you are hurt. Tell the universe that you feel bad and would like to stop feeling that way. This is a very wise thing to do, because the universe appreciates that you are mature enough to ask to feel good.

2. Release the situation or person who hurt you from the mix of emotions. Don't let the situation or person be drawn into the issue any more and let them be free to heal.

3. Take time to sit down and think. Process what happened, and if you still feel bad, ask that the situation be resolved.

4. If you still have anger and other negative emotions, just know that your energy will get you to take whatever action

is required to attain balance, even if it means educating the wrongdoer.

5. You can control the action you take so that it has a good outcome if you first process the issue and reduce its emotional impact. So heal as much as possible before you take action. The less hurt you feel, the more skillful your actions will be.

It is inevitable that your energy tries to balance itself as this world and its manifestations are always trying to attain balance. If you have been angry, then it means that it's time to be at peace. If you have been quiet to your detriment, then it's time to speak up.

The best way is to experience freedom in your heart before you take action, or you may act without a sense of direction. This is a world of emotions, and people carry baggage from their past. Sometimes anger and hurt do happen, but you have to release whatever happened and move on. Don't carry the negativity of your past into your next moment. Be free now.

In the state of freedom, all actions flow smoothly and are not tinged with worry, fear, regret, anger, and disillusionment. You are truly a master of your emotions; you rule your emotions and not vice-versa. Every action that you take flows so gracefully that it simply reaches out into space, touches others, and has positive outcomes. If you do end up acting without skill, that is okay, too. Forgive yourself, take time out, and bounce back with a smile. There is always a next time.

A positive space without hurt energy creates wonderful action.

From the previous point on attachment, you could ask the question, "What if something even worse than getting my car scratched happens and I feel really bad?

Negativity can happen, but by using the Joyful Manifestation process skillfully you can get into better energy so that things happen in your favor. For now, if you are witnessing a moment that is very hurtful to you, I ask you to do something; try to get into the gap between two hurtful thoughts and rest for a bit. Understand that this too shall pass. You don't have to deny your hurt feelings, but you can choose to be happy again, and allow for healing to happen.

Healing will happen and the moment of now, where you are suffering, will pass. The Self in you will not allow you to stay in sadness for long unless it is your personal choice to do so. Make the choice for joy, dear one, and you will see that whatever it is that you are suffering from will change and evolve. It has to. There is no other way.

Even if some loss happened that you feel you cannot cope with, I ask that you take every healthy opportunity to reconnect to your joy. Your life will change. In fact, even as you read these words, it is changing for the better. Believe it.

Whatever your hurt, you have picked up this book and others like it because the Self in you wants you to be happy and to succeed. Your Self feels that there is hope, so whatever your external situation, know this truth: your Self wants you to experience your joy again. You would not be reading this book if that were not the case. The blessings of so many masters, teachers, and angels are behind you right this minute. Feel their presence. So many enlightened ones have walked and are walking Earth right now. So many angels are watching; so many powerful beings want you to be happy. So don't wait anymore and start walking toward your joy. We are all with you. Your God Self is with you. Heal and be happy now.

4. INTENTION BEHIND MANIFESTATION

Intention fuels manifestation. What you intend directs the flow of your energy and the universal resources toward it. The universe is always supplying; it is constantly cooking something like a huge talented chef in action.

You are a part of the universe, the Mastermind behind the creation, and your intentions are a part of the making and unmaking, so be careful—you are the mind of the Chef. For example, if you feel bad about your job, then the universe receives this feeling as a request from you to get out of the job, and the next thing you know you are acting badly and arriving late at work, your boss then decides that he does not want you, and/or a situation arises where people start to get laid off.

It's your world. Nothing happens without your mental participation. So keep a lookout on your intentions, both conscious and unconscious.

As you form an intention to have something done, your energy gears up and actions flow accordingly. As you intend correctly—knowing what you really want—your actions start to align, and the information that comes to you from the universe will support your intentions.

A good example is of a woman who wants to become the next Miss Universe. Her desires and intentions will dictate what actions she takes. She will prepare for her role of becoming Miss Universe by making sure that she eats healthy foods, works out regularly, looks impeccable, and also acts in a way that is decent. She will not want to act in any way that she will have to feel embarrassed about. The extent of her intention will determine the skill with which she acts, on stage and off. If she only has a hazy dream, it will tell in her actions. If she is determined, however, she will make sure that her actions reflect that happy determination. Don't confuse determination with adverse attachment because if she gets overly attached to the title, she will create sleepless nights for herself and her actions will reflect her adverse attachment. She may become mean, and may not even enjoy the process of becoming Miss Universe.

So take care and intend, keeping your eye on the goal, free of adverse attachment.

Proper intention results in focused action.

5. ABILITY TO CHOOSE WISELY

When you are at a crossroads, and believe me, life can bring you several of these, it is time to fine tune your decision making abilities and learn how to make empowered choices.

The choices that you make decide your actions.

A crossroad indicates a fork. Standing at the tip of a fork, you have choices that determine your future course. The future scenery you will view depends on the road that you choose at the fork. Choose wisely, for you have only yourself to hold responsible for your choices. All kinds of forces may have worked to bring you to your current moment of decision, but what you do is still your choice. Center yourself in this moment of choice, and let the negative energy dissipate before you make your decision. It can determine the rest of your life.

Ask yourself:

"How does this choice make me feel?"

For example, there was a time in my life when I was influenced by other people's decisions and actions. I would wait with them in their space, persuading them to think and act differently. I spent years doing this without much benefit to me. My energy would get caught up in thinking about how the other person feels, why they wouldn't do what was good for them, and how I could get them to think in a manner more beneficial to them. The result was that my actions reflected my internal confusion and came out confused.

I finally understood that I was allowing others to affect my life, and that I was the only one responsible for my life's success. If I was getting caught up in trying to make someone do something, I was not helping anything or anyone. I learnt to keep on walking forward no matter what. My love was there for others, but I had to keep doing what I had to do, what I came here to do. I stopped the habit of waiting forever in other's spaces, persuading them to join me on my journey. I did wait just a bit, and then walked to a new space where they were free to join me if they wished (most people do join you if where you are is happy and feels good to them). This is a conscious choice I make when faced with crossroads.

You may face such situations in life and each choice of yours will play a role in creating your future. But then, it is your future, isn't it? It's not somebody else's, and it's your choices, so do make them carefully.

> *The right choice lays the ground for right action. Right action is that action which serves you in the long run and creates sustaining joy for you.*

Your preferences and choices create energy. When you prefer to buy clothes that are of a certain style, your manifestations happen from this space of preference. Choices are not only about huge issues, but also lifestyles. Just ask yourself: What do I prefer? And make your choices.

6. STRENGTH OF CONVICTION

The strength of your beliefs will determine the quality of your actions. How much power do you put behind your beliefs? Do you really believe that you will get what you want? If you believe good things about life, you will take the actions that prove you right.

+ If you believe that you sing really well, it will give you the courage to get up on stage, get a hold of the microphone, and sing.

+ If you believe that you can make it in a strange country with your education and talents, you will invest the required time and money, and make the move toward success.

Simply put, do you believe in what you want? Do you believe in yourself? How much conviction do you carry?

If your actions are graceful and carry conviction, you will be successful in your ventures. Gear up and convince yourself that you are amazing. The strength of the universe is with you so act from the space of this conviction.

Conviction fuels skilled action.

7. ABILITY TO BE CENTERED

Your core is the center of your world.

Being centered means resting in the core of you, which is joy and peace itself, and remaining undisturbed by events. Just like the planets in our solar system revolve around the Sun, which is the center of the solar system, your world revolves around your core. Your mind and body complex are also part of the world revolving around your core.

Away from the core of you, a lot of thought—action happens with various consequences, some good and some not so wonderful. Any action that you take from the space of these physical and mental happenings is tinged by those happenings and is influenced by them.

Any action that you take from the space of your core, which is peace and confidence itself, will carry that peace and confidence with it.

Being centered means moving away from the happenings of the physical and mental world and anchoring in your Core Self. Action taken from this space is powerful and loving, because the core of you is all-knowing, and really powerful. Your action will not be disturbed, because it did not flow from a disturbed place but came from a space that is so deep that to dive to the bottom would take forever. You are the *Self* at the core, and this Self knows how to think and act wisely to the best advantage of all concerned. So powerful, the core of you, so get centered.

> *Centered action will always be skillful action. Acting from your Core Self enables you to respond efficiently.*

8. ABILITY TO RESPOND EFFICIENTLY

The ability to respond to situations efficiently is a useful skill. Many people have good hearts and good intentions, but when it comes to responding efficiently to situations, they are somehow unable to do so. Learn how to respond to situations efficiently and you will not be stuck with regrets.

Take the CEO of a particular company. He dreamt of specific goals, aligned himself to his dreams, and became the CEO. Basically, he got what he wanted. His ability to respond to situations will be tested again and again, and he has to have the skills to respond efficiently. Before he became the CEO, he had to have experience and be the person who could handle situations and see them through to fruition. Having the responsibility that he does, the CEO has to fulfill them correctly.

> *The universe will only give you as much as you can handle. Learn the skills to handle situations, and be prepared to take on responsibility.*

When situations happen, are you able to respond efficiently? Do you fall apart? Do you get nervous? Even if you do get nervous (we all do), are you still able to act from the space of centeredness, or at least recover quickly?

Don't spend time lamenting and getting caught up in the how and why of each situation except to the extent of understanding the lessons so that you can do away with certain patterns of behavior. Regretting is not of much value, because it can keep your energy tied up in lower manifestation levels. Some regret is good to the extent that you realize what happened and your part in the situation. Once you incorporate the lesson in you, you will master yourself to that extent, and can let go of the happening, and take appropriate action.

Look at it this way. Let's say that you are caught in a hurricane. What are you going to do? You can only lament so much about why you are caught in it, or even your attraction factor that brought you into it. A much better solution is to take action. Spend time doing whatever has to be done to get out of the situation. Move into the energy of solutions, and do not continue to stay in the energy of the problem itself. A problem only perpetuates itself, while a solution brings in good news.

Be centered and take guided action and you will soon be out of the problem energy itself. When in a battle that represents the problem, keep your attention on the eye of the target and shoot (figuratively) so that you hit that eye. Do not get derailed by extraneous events. Again this is not about violence, but is about keeping your eye on the target and moving toward it with determination.

Anytime you are upset, first accept the situation, let go, and then get centered. Sometimes, however, your Self does allow you to be disturbed so that certain actions happen from what you think is the current reality. Sometimes even though you are peaceful, thoughts come up that make you do things that you may not normally do. In such times just surrender and know that the universe is getting you in place for what you want to see happen. This is not your action, but the action of your Self, which has its life to lead through you. It applies the forces required to get you to react in ways that can gets its job done. Such disturbed moments actually have a gift concealed in them, and if you remove the gift-wrap, you will see the gift inside. Just surrender and let the Self do what it wants, being just an instrument to the happening. Remember that truth is contradictory, and so even while things seem disturbed, be centered and feel strong and brave inside knowing that everything is in divine and perfect order.

Train yourself to become someone who can respond efficiently. As you become someone who is skilled at taking action and has the right intent behind his actions, the results that manifest will be good, taking you closer to Joyful Manifestation. Your ability of speech, persuasion, and action are all important. How you communicate information to people really matters, and a lot of your success rests on that.

Chapter Twenty–Five

~

Step 9: Allow

"I allow good in now."

Most of the work is done; releasing resistance, getting to a good space, and developing yourself, was the major work. Once this is done, you are in the space of allowing good in.

What does it mean to *allow*?

Most people run after things, and what they run after may run away from them. Similarly, what you run away from may run after you. What you resist persists to create your reality. Even if there is no physical 'running after' or 'running away' involved, energetically there is a push and pull indicating that you are pushing good away from you.

The very act of running after something means that it is not there with you. This is exactly why people get involved in one-sided love relationships and get walked over so often. They spend so much time trying to win a person's love against all odds, which can only work if you feel confident enough to do it. In most cases of one-sided relationships however, the level of confidence is so low after being rejected that winning someone over actually amounts to desperately running after and trying to get that person, which is counterproductive. You cannot 'get' someone; that someone has to meet you halfway.

Let's use the word 'flow' instead.

As you flow toward someone, that someone flows toward you.

Let's look at the phenomena behind one-sided love relationships:

1. Tom meets Jeannette and develops a liking for her.

2. He starts to visualize romantic situations and a future with her.

3. Jeannette is able to feel the desire also, but she may or may not show it yet.

4. If Jeannette does show interest, Tom feels good and pursues her.

5. However, if Jeannette is not aware of her feelings so she does not show interest yet or that she is aware, but is bound by physical circumstances from showing her interest. What happens then?

6. Tom starts to feel restless as his attention is not being met halfway. He starts to get into the energy of push and pull. He either pushes Jeannette for an answer or sabotages whatever possibilities exist by hurting her. Love-hate emotions start to flood Tom's mind. Unable to cope with this, he develops sadness, anger and depression.

7. By now, Jeanette is so turned off by this drama that she backs away, adding more fuel to the fire.

Stop Tom. Take a breather. Focus your attention toward creating happiness and success in other life areas. Stop this push and pull. Rest, will you?

Whenever push and pull happens, good energy is not allowed in naturally. It is important to come to a state of rest first. When at rest, the mind is free and the Self comes up with positive manifestation visions, creating new attraction vibrations. It also sends up ingenious ideas. After all, it is the Source of everything. When the mind is at rest, the heart feels secure and opens its gates for what you really want to come in.

When the heart feels good, allowing happens.

Whenever you are caught in situations, practice the steps of Joyful Manifestation and get back into the space of *allowing* what you really want to flow to you. Go toward joyful situations, and flow with that joy because your heart controls what comes in and what does not. It is a precious part of you, and you must take good care of it, so give it healthy and happy situations, and it will open up and allow good in.

Some points on allowing:

1. You start to allow something in as soon as you like it.

2. Any thought in your mind that is *against* what you want to create stops you from allowing it in. It acts like an energy door that closes against the flow of allowing.

3. When you feel joy even once about a subject matter, allowing happens automatically until you create another reason for stopping what you want.

4. Navigate energy carefully, and find out if you are allowing or disallowing what you want from coming to you.

5. When you really like something and feel joy, a door opens in the universe that allows what you like in. If what you want creates stress, resistance builds up and what you want cannot come in.

6. Remove your resistances in order to allow what you want into your life. Resistances are thought forms that tell you a story that you think is true, stopping what you want from coming to you.

7. Tell yourself another story. Give yourself new possibilities. Allow.

Chapter Twenty–Six

~

Step 10: Receive and Maintain

"I receive graciously, and I maintain what I receive, with love."

Once you are in the space of solutions, you are already in the place of being ready to receive. All you have to do is to remove resistances and allow things to come your way. Make sure that your walls are down, or at least low enough so that what you asked for comes through with speed, and then receive it. All that you're required to do is remain in the mode (or mood) of allowing good in.

We now come to the next important point. Many times people ask for and are given something, but they don't maintain what they have been given. People are so used to being Master Unmanifesters that they find it hard to remain in the space of good vibrations. For example, there are many who ask for love, but after they receive it, they find it hard to maintain that love. In the same way, when one is endowed with beauty and good health, it is imperative that these be maintained in their original state of good. Many countries are experts at constructing beautiful buildings and monuments, but do they maintain them? Do they maintain their buildings and roads in good and clean conditions? This world was given in a good condition, yet it is now being flooded with garbage, plastic, and toxic wastes.

Maintaining and building upon whatever God has already given you is a skill in itself. It is as important to learn this skill as the method of initial creation. Everything needs to be maintained in good order and if something that you have received, whether on an individual or world level, starts to fall into disarray, follow the Joyful Manifestation process again and bring it back into good health.

In fact, it is better to keep an eye out and not wait for it to start to fall into disarray. Just like you would keep up the maintenance of your home before it fell into disrepair and cost you a lot of money, it is a good practice to maintain what you have received from the universe in good condition. Always align yourself with the complete picture of well-being for everything and everyone that is precious to you.

Emotions that are in balance keep you in balance, and keep your manifestations in balance, and good health. Try to keep your emotions healthy for yourself and your loved ones. Being centered is necessary for maintaining what you have, and what you will receive. If the universe finds that you are not able to maintain what has already been given to you, it can take it away. You cannot then blame the universe, because after all, everything is created from within you. It is your universe.

What should you do if you have not been alert in maintaining what has been given to you?

1. Discover if you still want to continue your active enjoyment of it.

2. Speak to God, your Self and the universe with earnestness, and profess your thankfulness for what is already there.

3. Even though things may have fallen into disarray now, ask for how you would like for it to be. Visualize what you want feeling good about the future.

4. Allow realizations to come up from within you. You may have to swallow some pride and allow your ego to relax as you incorporate new lessons into your consciousness.

5. With this new awareness, ask for opportunities for making changes.

6. Follow the steps of Joyful Manifestation, and this time around, be prepared to fully treasure what the universe has so generously given you.

You have been given so much—enjoy it fully. You deserve your rewards and deserve to attract more abundance into your life. The steps for Joyful Manifestation create powerful vibrations that align you with the thoughts, actions, and deeds of some of the best in this world. As you use the Joyful Manifestation process to attract what you want, you will get better at manifesting.

There is additional information on the subjects of money and romantic love covered in the next two chapters that will help with the successful manifestation of these two life areas.

Chapter Twenty–Seven

~

Soul Mate and Other Relationships

"And I meet the one who mirrors me in my perfection and my imperfections; just myself in another body."

The information in this chapter is the result of working with hundreds of people and their situations with positive results. Of course each person is unique and so each individual situation is unique, but this information can be used to bring about positive change in most relationships.

Even though you should use the steps detailed in the Joyful Manifestation process to manifest what you want, keep the following information in mind because it is particular to love relationships, especially soul mate. Your soul is here to experience love in different forms, whether it is parental love, sibling love, love from children, love from your employers, and love from friends and society. In a way each person that plays an important role in your life is a kind of a soul mate to you, so this information can be used to work out your love karma with almost anyone.

What is love karma?

LOVE KARMA

For any relationship to prosper, your love karma needs to be good, whether romantic or otherwise.

Your love karma is very important. Your love karma is your ability to get love and to keep it flowing consistently while enjoying it fully. It is your ability to give and receive love without fear of loss, rejection and abandonment.

My question to you; are you having a problem with your experience of love?

Well breathe easy because you are not alone in this. Almost everyone has a problem with this life area. There are millionaires and billionaires who struggle with this life area even though they may have mastered other important life areas, like money and work. Rich people, poor people, beautiful people, not so beautiful people, people with light skin, people with dark skin, people from the United States of America, from Europe and other parts of the world, people from advanced countries, people from so-called third world countries, people of this century and people from past centuries, film stars, politicians, business people, musicians, and everyone else, are all busy trying to get love, to keep it and to enjoy it in its various forms and flavors.

Your love karma may be rock solid right now, down in the dumps, or even somewhere in the middle. If your love karma is really good right now, congratulations, but if it is not that good, or even if you would like to just maintain it in continued good health, please continue reading.

Your energy contains important information about your love karma; loss, joy, confidence, sexual satisfaction, lack, abundance, good experiences and bad experiences; everything is stored in your energy which beeps out messages attracting people and situations to you. In each life you get to rid yourself of your negative love karma and keep the positive karma, building more and more on it.

> *Your soul mate reflects your love karma, and will bring out the best and the worst in you to observe and to change.*

YOUR SOULMATE

What happens when you meet the special one? Most people don't know what hit them when they meet someone who could be a soul mate. The term soul mate has been explained in many ways over many years, but I am most comfortable with this one.

> *A soul mate is someone who mirrors you and is there to experience life with you. Whether you make it for the rest of the life or not depends a lot on the understanding that both of you get into on the spiritual level, and your ability to work things out on the physical level.*

When you meet someone who is a soul mate you will start a spiritual journey that can take you beyond all that you have experienced till date.

Here are some of the common soul mate scenarios, there are several other permutation and combinations that can happen, but the following are the most common ones that people experience.

1. Boy meets girl, boy likes girl, girl does not like boy immediately, makes it difficult for the boy to get her, and thus starts a karmic journey.

2. Boy meets girl, boy likes girl, girl likes boy, then an ex or spouse arrives on the scene and there is trouble in paradise.

3. Boy meets girl, boy likes girl, girl seems to like boy, shows it partially, then pulls away, does not commit, and there starts a push and pull journey.

4. Boy meets girl, boy likes girl, girl likes boy, but suddenly boy finds out that his ex in the meantime had his baby. Oops.

5. Boy meets girl, boy likes girl, girl likes boy, they make it to the finish line, get married, and then starts a karmic journey as all their issues, until then seemingly hidden or manageable, hit the ceiling.

Relationshp rules or manifestation laws?

Do any of the above situations sound familiar to you? Do you recognize any of the above situations as being close to yours and what do you do when you encounter such situations?

Decide to handle this life area as a manifestation project and stop the push and pull on your side immediately. Go by manifestation laws and not by relationship rules.

For example relationship rules state that your man should treat you at least as good as you treat him, if not better. If you go by relationship rules, your man may fall short almost all of the time and you may want to leave him. There are many relationship rules that he may break, each one pushing you to stop wanting him. If you treat this as a manifestation project instead, you can use the laws of manifestation to work with the energy to change the various negative attraction points and the negative love karma that you may have.

The Joyful Manifestation process is complete in itself to help you manifest whatever you want, but where soul mate relationships are concerned it is good to keep the following soul mate manifestation tips in mind. The information is much more than just tips but since I am not putting them into a separate process but instead stating them as points, I refer to them as tips. Please continue to use the Joyful Manifestation process for the actual manifestation process itself.

Some of what I have written below may make you feel less empowered as a woman or man, but if you look into each individual point, even though on the surface it may not seem empowering, yet it empowers you from deep within as you realize that you can last longer in the soul mate race, and not have to beat your soul mate over his head just to show him that you are empowered, or the other extreme, be a doormat.

Okay let's start.

What do you do when you meet your special one? For the sake of convenience I will refer to the woman as you, and the man as the soul mate we are working with.

1. **Take it Easy**

    After you meet your special someone, try to keep calm and know that this love story can twist and turn crazily before it reaches its final destination. You don't know what you are in for! Here is a man that can send you to the moon and back, and then send you on another journey to Mars with a one way ticket, while he decides if he is going to abandon you there, or send a rescue ship to bring you back.

    Fighting with the man will not help in most cases; remember that if he is your soul mate then he is **at least** as strong as you, if not stronger. Allow him to show you what he wants and don't push or pull.

    Please don't have any expectations beyond what he shows you in any moment. What he shows you may keep you entranced while wanting to pull your hair at the same time, but you may still have to go with the pace he is setting, while making your adjustments through energy. You can stand up for yourself as required, and he will appreciate it, but use logic instead of high emotions and you will get through to him better. Make most of your moves in a skillful way, and work with the energy to speed things up, if you must.

2. You are connected

You are connected to your soul mate by energy cords. Energy keeps travelling through these cords and so you must monitor your thoughts and feelings about your soul mate, because he can get them all. Just when you least expect it, he may flood you with his thoughts and feelings and leave you feeling either tingly or in pain, depending on what he is going through. You can cut these cords, but they will most likely grow back when you think of him again.

3. Sexual energy

How strong is your sexual energy and how good is it? Have you shut down everything sexual about you for many years and waiting for your soul mate to heal you? Sometimes your soul mate might have the same issue as you but expressed in a different way. Heal your sexuality and become aware of this important part of you. Your sexual energy needs to flow healthily. This is not about sleeping around all the time, but doing what you need to do to keep your sexual energy alive and healthy, that is of becoming aware that you are also a sexual being.

4. Let go of the neediness and hurt

Don't show him that you are needy by contacting and pursuing him more than he does you. Neediness energy shows that you don't believe that your man loves you truly, and is an affirmation that goes into the universe bringing back yet more reasons to be needy and insecure.

It is good to stop getting hurt every time he does something to upset you because he may not stop his negative behavior until you stop the negative attraction factor for hurt.

I have people ask me very frequently; "Does he not know that he hurts and causes me pain? Why does he keep causing me pain if he loves me?"

> ### *It's upto you to stop getting hurt and feeling pain all the time. It's upto you to stop the suffering.*

You have an attraction factor for hurt and pain, and he is the tool causing it again and again. At some level you enjoy the hurt and the pain because if you don't really enjoy it, you would stop feeding into it. It's just like watching sad movies and crying, or watching horror movies and experiencing fear. You like them, even if you don't admit that you do. The drama gives you something to feel alive about.

> ### *Here is a news flash for you- feeling joy also is a measure of being alive.*

The truth is that if you really wanted to stop suffering, you would. You would find the man so funny with his crazy habits of pushing you away, that you would probably hold your sides and laugh till you cry; at least this type of crying is good.

What you resist does persist. Asking him to stop causing you pain may not work, so just turn difficult situations into laughter. If the man keeps doing the same things, throwing the same stones at you, throwing the same irritating other women at you, it is time to laugh at his antics and not let it bother you. Turn every stone he throws at you into a flower and wear it in your hair. Maybe he is just trying to make you jealous. Either way, it is important to stop the suffering otherwise you will just attract more negativity.

5. Don't turn cold and freeze up

While it is a good practice to not be needy, the other opposite of turning cold and not being open to take the first step at all is also not a good idea. If you freeze up because of all the disappointments you have experienced with him, it will not help in your manifestation and so it is good to be flexible and be willing to take some guided action from time to time.

While it is good to maintain your dignity, it is not good to act from false ego. Once you let go of the false ego, action that you take out of your good nature will not have the stamp of neediness on it.

> *Be careful whether your action comes from neediness or simply from the fact that you are a wonderful person and are acting according to your nature.*

6. Children are not insurance policies against a breakup

To maintain any relationship in good health, it is important that you base your relationship on true love. Please don't get pregnant only to keep your man. It may work for some time, but may not work for all time. Children are just that, children, and are here for their own lives, not to create your love relationship. It is true that children can help bond parents with a common goal, but sooner or later the truth of your relationship with your partner will be seen and so it is best to base your relationship purely on how you get along with your partner.

7. Don't force commitment

Commitment is not a prison so please don't ask for a commitment from day one. If a man enters a marriage but does not feel real love for his woman, nothing can keep him committed. True commitment is when he loves you so much that he doesn't need any other woman.

Asking for a commitment without being the woman that he really wants to be with is not going to work because you cannot force commitment on someone. That someone will commit only when he really wants to commit. Your soul mate could value his independence and if he feels tied down, he will fight you. His true commitment comes from his love for you, and from his desire to be with you and to continue experiencing you and only you.

8. Avoid drama

If trouble comes up, avoid arguments and self-righteous behavior to the maximum extent possible. I hear statements like "If he really loved me, why does he behave the way he does". The answer is – He may love you, but it may not be time to show you that love because something in you still needs to be fine tuned. When you do that, he will show you love the way you really want.

You can't push, pull, fight and argue your way into someone's heart. Emotional drama is just that- drama. It cannot hold someone's love and attention for long. Sooner or later, everything will hit the ceiling and you will be left holding nothing.

If he is divorced or has been/is in a relationship, don't remind him of his ex/his other woman. If she was/is a drama queen, try not to be one. Try not to be possessive and give the man his space. However don't go to the other extreme and fear him. It's ok to respect someone and not behave badly, but please don't do the exact opposite and fear him either. Learn how to say 'no' politely, when required, to bad behavior. Be brave and speak up when required keeping in mind the effect of what you say to him, on him. Try not to become the other woman in his life because you may end up in that position for a very long time.

9. **Work with your soul mate, not against him**

Remember that your soul mate is here to help you get to the state of absolute confidence. You may have brought into this life imprints of loss, hurt, grief, deceit, being cheated on, lied to, being shy, scared, etc. Your soul mate will bring out all these doubts and fears in you and you get a chance to clear these negative imprints from your energy. Your soul mate will do whatever it takes, and behave in whichever way needed so that your worst fears come out to stare you in the face, and bite you in places you never knew existed. As you attain the state of absolute love and confidence in yourself and eliminate states of neediness, despair and depression, your soul mate will reflect the positive changes in you, by making changes in his behavior. Listen to what he says, learn quickly from his hints and take mental notes because things you remember now may come in handy later.

> *Even as you go about changing yourself for the relationship, maintain balance. The ability to say 'no' when required will help you.*

10. **He is your mirror**

When a soul mate is said to mirror you, it means that he is a mirror to who you are at any point. He will show you, like a mirror, the positive and the negative in full living color. He will reflect your insecurities and your true self-worth at any time. Until you arrive at your feeling of wholeness and completion, you may be subject to the worst criticism, the worst forms of rejection, and the feeling that you are just not worth his time and attention. These are extreme cases and most situations reflect a mild to medium form of the same. The goal is to increase your self-worth and know that nobody but you is the obvious choice for him because there is no-one better than you, for him. As you arrive at this conclusion, and hold it steadily, your soul mate will start to reflect it to you.

You are here to experience yourself and your soul mate is the mirror to your beauty. As you realize who you are, so does your soul mate. Everything you do is just to get you to believe that you are truly wonderful and have him and life reflect this back to you.

For example, let's say that you are not monetarily well to do and your man is not impressed, you may want to move onto someone who thinks less of money, but you may not be able to forget this particular man. What should you do?

Work hard and become successful, nobody loses; it's a win-win situation. As you get motivated and start to think of yourself more confidently, he feels that confidence, you attract him and everyone is happy. It is important to not feel resentful of the mental and physical work you have to put in to get the man, the man is your soul mate and he was supposed to get you into abundance and help you feel good about yourself.

There can be times when you pull a man into your mess with you, but if he is your real soul mate, he will push you to do better instead of allowing himself to suffer with you; he will force you to bring about changes in your life. This does not mean that you are not worthy of his attention just as you are, but that your soul wants you to get out of your messy life. A good example is of this woman who was in debt and met her soul mate, a man who held a high career position and did well monetarily. He liked her, but still decided to walk away. My client went through this inner urge to do better, and as she rose up in her career, she got the man back.

Your viewpoint on this may be that the man did not love her genuinely for who she was, whether rich or poor and that she should have gotten rid of him. Look at this way, after she met this man, she got motivated to work hard and do very well professionally and monetarily. She felt proud of herself, and when the time was right, the universe allowed the man back into her life to mirror her success. He always had the seed of love for her, but that seed was not allowed to mature until she changed and achieved her soul goals.

Another example is of an emotional woman who always reacted badly to insults. She met a man and he never showed her that he loved her, let alone wanted anything from her. A few years later, she met the same man, and being more emotionally stable, the man told her how he truly felt about her.

Ultimately, it does not matter if you are rich or poor, but depending on who you attract, you will know what to do and how to grow. Every dollar you earn, every gym class you attend, all emotional growth, maturity and stability you achieve, everything you do to improve yourself, is all for you to become the best you. If you are shy, you will be made to open up, if you are afraid of sex you will start to enjoy your body (safely), if you are lazy you will become more active and if you like alcohol, you will feel motivated to clean up your act.

Your soul mate's consciousness supports and balances you and vice versa. Both of you bring something to the table that the other did not have. You can actually be saved from severe life problems and illnesses if your soul mate balances you out properly. He can bring you wealth, happiness, good health and self-empowerment if he is the right man for you. A really good example is of this man who saw all his brothers succumb to one of those major diseases. He also got that disease but managed to get out of that disease and become well because his soul mate had no evidence of that disease in her family genes. Her consciousness, which was free of this disease, managed to support his consciousness, and he survived.

11. He may be your mirror but you are your own barometer

What this means is that even as your soul mate is your mirror reflecting you perfectly, yet he can only reflect what you feel within you. You are the barometer to where you truly are in life. For example, if you feel that your hair is not at its best on a particular day and that you are feeling tired, try looking into a mirror. The mirror can only reflect what you think of your hair; it may show you that your face is tired, and that your hair is looking flat.

Check how you feel about yourself before you look at your soul mate for confirmation. If you only look at your soul mate and don't feel good yourself, you may not have the good experience you seek from him.

12. Changing your love karma is your job, not his

Questions like why should I work on this while he/she does nothing should be kept aside. This is your life, you are the center of your universe and it is you mastering the life area of love, so yes, the task falls on you to work with the Joyful Manifestation process. Your soul mate will respond to whatever changes you bring about in your consciousness, and will mirror you. Use the Joyful Manifestation process to keep changing the energy level so that you get closer to what you want. Visualize the kind of life you want with him, create it in your mind, and see him in it. As you mentally create a good life together, he starts to have access to the energy of the life you created with him in your mind. This is your love karma scenario and he is only playing a role.

One question I regularly come across is- Should I leave this relationship? Should I forget about him? This is too difficult for me.

The man you are in love with is the current
face of your soul mate. Change as much of
your love karma with him, as possible.

Work on your love karma with your current soul mate and if
you really want him for the rest of your life, ask the universe
for him. Most times if you leave a situation too early, you may
just have to continue it with someone else.

13. Persistence pays

You can either want the man because you want marriage and/
or a baby, or want the man for who he really is. Decide on what
you want and put your intention behind it. Those who want the
marriage and the baby just because they want to get married
and become a parent may settle for people who are not their
real soul mates.

There is no right or wrong here, it is your choice. I have worked
with people who say "It is him or nobody else!" and they mean
it. When they work with the process correctly, they can end up
happy with the man of their heart. However if any man will do,
this will be reflected in the energy and the soul mate may either
move on or keep up with the difficult behavior as he knows that
he is not truly loved. Your man will know if you are flighty in
nature or if you are solid inside and out.

Even if you have spent ten years waiting for this man, but start
working with the right information now, you may see healthy
changes happening.

Keep your eye on the energy, and not on time.
Stop counting months because in any fight with
time, time will win. This is because energy
cannot develop and be established in the high

vibration required for positive manifestation if you are stressed about the time it takes.

14. If he is negative, be the positive person

Don't give in to his sadness, if any, and don't buy into his sad stories. Continue down your happy path of success. If he is negative about the relationship, take charge of the manifestation. Someone has to keep faith. He could be having his own negative karma going on, and if you can maintain the positive side of this, everyone will be served.

15. Communication karma

At some point in your relationship with your soul mate, you may go through what I call "communication karma". This is when he stops calling you, stops talking to you, or calls or talks to you in brief spurts. This can send you into total panic as you feel your relationship slipping away from you as distance builds up. In terms of energy, what this means is that the energy flow of words either stops completely, or it reduces into a trickle, with a stop and start quality to it. Energy needs to have words in it, for communication to happen. It cannot happen when he does not know what to say to you. Your communication can also have angry words, meaning bad communication.

What do you do?

a. For some time let go of the need to hear from your loved one. If you get disturbed by the communication karma, you will only add to the negative energy. Completely suspend all expectations to hear from the person concerned.

b. Telepathically connect to your loved one's energy and speak to him. Depending on how you speak to him, the energy starts to improve because words are being infused into the energy and his consciousness starts responding to you.

Help him deal with any blocks that might have developed. Your physical communication will improve as your energy communication improves.

c. If the communication energy is hurt because of lack of trust, insults, etc., heal the hurt energy and don't add to it. As his energy starts to trust you again, you will see your physical communication improve. Your physical communication will depend on how well you establish energy communication.

d. If you have made it difficult for him to communicate with you, he may not do so because he may not want a drama queen. You cannot improve your communication if you are frustrated. Drop your frustration and become calm. Stop your energy from pushing him either mentally or physically. If your energy is busy pushing him, he will either withdraw or push back.

e. Use communication discreetly and take guided physical action, at the right time, in the right way. Yes, he may love you, but may not show it yet. Work patiently and win the physical evidence of that love.

f. Communication should have purpose. For example if you have been friends for some time and the relationship is supposed to evolve to another level, one partner may suspend communication until the other one gets that this is no friendship but is actually a romantic relationship. The foundation of all communication is purpose and your soul mate should have reason to talk to you. The common question I get is "Why doesn't he call me?" He won't call you unless he has reason to call you. The initial reasons for flirting, etc., may be exhausted and he may need more reasons. Build up the reasons in your mind; are you his wife? Do you think you have a future together? Do you think he enjoys talking to you because you are so joyful? Work on your purpose, and change your communication karma.

16. Work with positive universal forces

The positive forces of the universe want you to have what you desire and are always helping you. Work with these forces and consciously ask them for help. They include the angels, and other universal helpers. Seek their help to send messages, and to protect your loved one(s). As you work with the positive forces of the universe, you will start to see more happy coincidences.

Sometimes these positive forces create an energy curtain between you and your loved one, not allowing him to come to you until you release your blocks, evolve and realize your true self-worth in a loving manner. It may then lift the curtain when the time is right allowing you to see happy evidence that what you want is coming to you.

17. Neutralize negative forces

The negative forces on the other hand may create artificial situations either preventing your loved one from seeing your messages, occupying him in other tasks, distracting him, or simply muddling his mind keeping him either confused or angry. In such situations, work to increase positive energy in the situation and trust that good will happen. Work with the Joyful Manifestation process.

Remember that there is negative energy and sometimes this negative energy can create artificial blocks between you and your loved one. While it is better not to focus on the negative energy, if negative things are happening, at least know why. If someone does not respond immediately to your texts and email, know that the negative forces of the universe are out and are interfering with your love life. They know how to build energy walls so that your messages either don't go through, he is kept distracted, or his mind is being played with to make him moody. Don't blame him, blame the negative forces. He is not your enemy, the negative forces are.

Learn to distinguish between a person's personality, and the play of negativity in the situation. If you like the person, and are puzzled by why a person behaves like that with you, especially if things were good at the start, then it is the play of negativity.

> ## *Most negative forces start interfering more when you get closer to victory.*

It was time for you to succeed, and the negative forces decide to bring you down. Learn to recognize this pattern as it occurs and decide not to be pushed off your path.

Sometimes the negative forces can also bring you past soul mates and future possible affairs just to distract you from your goals. If you get involved with their energies, it can make things difficult, so be careful about the preferences you put out into the universe.

> ## *Soul mate energies don't mix and one energy can push the other one out. Learn to focus and remove all distractions unless you really want the new person(s). Decide what and who you really want. Your preferences matter.*

For example, if your current soul mate, the person you really want has not yet declared his love, you may manifest another man who may treat you well initially, just enough for you to get distracted and lose your real soul mate. This new man's colors may change later. Each situation is unique and you must find out who your real soul mate is. Be careful while you make your choices.

18. Resolve Other Woman Karma (or Other Man Karma)

This is very common. You love someone and just when you think things are okay, another woman pops up on the scene. Maybe you had warning signs or maybe you did not. Either way, you can certainly do something about it. This woman may be a wife, an ex or someone completely new.

Remember the Joyful Manifestation process. You are the Sun, you are the center of your universe and it is upto you to get empowered so that you can keep your man revolving in your universe around you. If you lose your power to anything or anybody, he will fly off to revolve around the other person and you will be left standing wondering what happened.

Here are some points to keep in mind while dealing with this negative karma.

a. The other woman is not really your enemy even though you may think that she is your enemy. Somehow, somewhere you lost focus of 'who' you really are and she drifted in and took over. In such situations you cannot fight, push or pull. You can only become a better version of yourself. You just have to get more empowered, and stop losing your power to every Jill, Jane and Janet that passes by.

b. Take stock of where you are and what thoughts you think; are you focusing too much on the man to your detriment, or the opposite; are you not treating him well? Are you jealous by nature? Are you insecure? Do you not think that you are the best there is in this world and that after God made you, he decided that he cannot create a more perfect human specimen?

c. Have you stopped focusing on your personal success? How is your money doing? How are your health and your food habits? Have you forgotten yourself and your goals?

d. Are you busy looking at his social media pages following up on what he is doing, what pictures he puts up, and of whom? What about your social media page; does it show you in a positive light? Whose social media page has more energy, and of what quality is it?

e. Are you watching his life story? His life story especially with the other woman in it is like a bad movie. Why would you watch that movie? Turn that movie off and instead make your life story wonderful. Make it fun, happy and exciting. As you stop watching his movie and are more interested in yours, he will feel it and turn his attention to your life story because quite frankly your story is much more exciting than his.

f. For some time as this other woman revolves around him, his energy may be toxic to you. It is important that you learn to tune out this toxic energy, and just try to remember him all alone and wonderful the way he was when you first fell in love with him. No doubt you have some nice memories. Access those wonderful memories and forget the toxic aspect of your soul mate for some time. As you learn to focus on the wonderful memories of him, he will detoxify and become safe for you to be with.

g. Once the other woman energy manifests in your life, it will be toxic to you. The other woman's energy will know if her man likes someone else and may try to bring you down. Completely block out her energy and focus on your personal success. Pay attention while working, driving, and while taking care of yourself and your family because negative energy can be at its peak during this time and can affect you. Stop tuning into it. Don't think of her, and ignore her very existence. Sooner or later she will unmanifest because if you don't focus on her, and just focus on your life, she will disappear as she becomes redundant.

h. If he is already in another relationship with this other woman, it is good to create an imaginary partnership for him to transfer to. He may love you, but he needs to know what he is getting; a new partnership that will be beneficial to him.

A million dollar question people have is "If he really loves me, why can't he choose me over her?" He may love you, but he will also look at how much his life is being disrupted by the change of partnership. You must be a winning proposition for him to make that move. Don't feel bad about yourself but instead be aware of what you bring to the table.

I can hear you saying "But what is he bringing to me?" I am sure that at some level you already know the answer to this question otherwise you would not want him. Remind yourself of the positive he brings to the situation and feel good.

i. Try to understand your true purpose in his life and don't take him away from someone else just for the fun of it. Are you really good for him? Did he change positively after meeting you? Are you able to show him light? Are you good for his evolution? Will his life extend healthily because of you?

As you gain understanding of why you are good for him, your vibrations will improve for the better and the truth will be reflected back to you, as he too realizes the reasons he should be with you.

j. There are some stages you will experience as you move through the other woman or man karma-

    a) Discovery and denial of the other person.

    b) Fear of the other person and what it can do to your relationship.

    c) Confrontation either directly or with the energy of the other person. This is where you get into your warrior mode. Avoid it if you can.

d) Ignoring the other person. This is where you finally get that it is far better to ignore the other person and that if you do it successfully, she will go away.

e) Working on yourself to create positive energy. Your energy shines brightly for your man to feel good about you.

19. Resolve Loss Karma

You are consciousness and have lived many lives. Losses you suffered are brought forward into this life in your energy and may cause you to attract more. It is important to work on your loss karma as you need to clear it.

For example, I have done sessions with people whose spouses went off into war and never came back, in past lives, and immediate pasts also. This created emotional imprints of loss carried forward into current lives, manifesting as energy blocks preventing soul mates from coming together in love, and staying together. The man may have fear of losing his life while the woman may go through the fear of losing him.

If such blocks exist, work on yourself and know that this life could be different. Send mental messages to your soul mate telling him that he is safe and nothing negative will happen to him.

20. Harness actual psychic energy

Don't always get stuck in the information of things, rather get into the feeling of things. Even as you learn to think better and become really good at it, it remains theoretical until you harness the actual psychic energy behind situations. For example, you can affirm that your man loves you, and wants you, and even feel good about it, but can you also **feel** that he is watching you and is observing everything you do? Okay I know this screams stalker mentality, but without your man being really interested in you, you cannot have him. So it is good to think that he keeps an eye on you and also feel his energy presence around you. This will bring his energy into your physical world. Ready his room or his side of the closet for him, and think of what you will buy for him when he does turn up. Walk as if he were by your side, giving you everything you always wanted; the perfect dance, the perfect dinner, and the perfect life.

Psychics measure the presence of a type of energy in your aura and tell you about it, but energy can change and predictions may or may not happen. Still it is good to know what type of energy you are attracting so that you can work on it. Mere information of the Law of Attraction without harnessing psychic energy through correct thinking and feeling may not be of much use to you.

Keep your soul mate's energy going by feeling it into existence.

There is a fine line between actively engaging in your man's energy, and being needy. Always focus on your personal success and don't get needy. If you find that you are getting needy to your detriment, refocus attention onto your life.

21. Use Telepathy

Soul mates are connected telepathically and they feel each other. While one person may be more intuitive, yet both have some idea of how the other person feels from time to time. If you feel that your man is angry with you, you can connect to him in your mind and talk to him. Explain how you feel and give him your point of view. He will understand and change his energy accordingly, helping you get into a positive space. Don't bully him, just be nice.

22. Visualize, dream away

Create your life the way you want it. Imagine a good life with him with sufficient details. Imagine into existence your house and your activities with him. Sometimes your soul mate may not have knowledge of his future with you because he may not have access to the energy of that future yet. Create the energy of your future together so that he can access it, and modify his behavior toward you accordingly.

As you change your love karma, and the energy of your relationship, new energy will surround him and enter his mind. He will also send out energy that surrounds you and enters your mind. If you don't like the energy he sends, telepathically tell him that. Your words will help to change the prevalent energy and he will respond accordingly.

Your soul mate is yours to work with. Look forward to enjoying a happy life with him.

Chapter Twenty-Eight

~

Money Manifestation

"I attract more than enough money to have the lifestyle I want. Money flows easily to me."

The whole world runs on money. To do most things you need money; you need to have purchasing power.

Money is a very interesting subject. For years it was viewed as dirty and the root of all evil. So many stories were written with money as the object of desire, where people cheated, robbed, and killed to become rich. You may have read stories of slums and rich land lords taking from the poor and building empires on their grief.

Money is not the root of all evil. Money is a resource to be used to take care of what you love; your health, your family and your country, to provide yourself with luxuries that make you feel good.

Money is a double edged sword, and can be used either for good, or bad. How you use money and what you do to get it, depends on you; it is upto you to define your relationship with money.

Money is energy

Sometimes there is absence of money in a person's life and sometime's there is the presence of money. The actual currency; the dollar, pound, etc., is the physical form of the energy of money. You cannot have hard cash in hand if you don't have the energy of money in your aura.

The space around you should be alive with money energy. When the air around you becomes thick with money, you will sense it. If someone is in lack or poverty, the space is probably empty of money energy and when this happens, the person cannot grasp that there is money around him. His mind may search for money energy and come up empty.

Your job is to get the energy of money flowing thickly in your space, and make ways for it to come into your life in physical form, like starting a business, getting better employment, etc.

This world depends on you

Getting money energy into your life is important. The reason it is important other than for your own personal reasons, is to bring about more abundance into this world. It makes the job of the people involved in the creation of money, easier. Yes there are people in this world devoted entirely to the making of money and all its decisions, and it is imperative that you also help because it helps your world get into better economic condition. It helps shift it into wealth and abundance, instead of getting into poverty, of which there is some danger.

Wealth or poverty can happen on an individual level, country level or world level and you can help create wealth on all levels. There is a money maker in you and all you have to do is activate it to contribute to the creation of wealth. To do this however, your beliefs about money should be sound.

Your beliefs about money makes a difference

Do you find money interesting in a good way? What do you personally believe about wealth, abundance, enjoying luxury, and having a good time? Do you like big houses, good décor, grand hotels with luxury evident everywhere? Do you like good food and clothing, or do you have a minimalistic approach? Ofcourse there are people who have simple tastes but still like making money for the sake of money itself, to be financially secure in life. I want to club them with the group that likes wealth and all that it represents no matter what their personal tastes are like because wanting abundant financial security is a part of this. There are various levels of wealth and luxury enjoyment and no matter what level you choose, you still form a part of the group that believes in a good life.

I have a question for you. When you read the above did you feel like shivering as if what I wrote spanked so much of debauchery and waste? Do you now feel like writing to me and telling me about starving children and the many parts of the world that are in dark poverty, while I talk about gross wealth?

Check your mind and how it thinks because in there is your money code and the key to your personal wealth.

Here is another possible belief you can check. Do you feel bad when you hear about the multi-millionaires and billionaires who attract so much wealth that they don't know what to do with it?

Most of them worked hard to get their wealth. Many of them have businesses that actually provide people with work and sources of income. Many of them had hard lives working hours that most people cannot handle, using their minds in ways that most people cannot imagine. If they sit pretty on top of mountains of money today, it's because they worked for it (exceptions always exist). They overcame their insecurities, were open to ridicule and probably failed many times before they became who they are. Notwithstanding how they manage their businesses (the laws of karma knows how to handle that) still most of them continue to work hard even today.

It's good to learn something from them rather than hate them. If you have been at the mercy of the economy and job markets till today, it is now upto you to make yourself secure either with improved skills that ensure that nobody can overlook you in the job market, or by starting your own business.

If everyone created wealth energy and ushered in abundance mindset, it would improve economic situations for people in general. The real good you can do for this world is to bring in abundance consciousness. My job here is not to make you into someone who has a conscience; I already assume that you do. My job is to help you open up the doors to the kind of wealth that you imagine would be good for you to experience, and then some more. There are healthy ways to make money providing services and goods that can help the world. You can attract great wealth to you while providing the means for others to make that wealth also.

> *The stage is yours to perform on dear one, and the universe is here to support you. Anything that you can imagine into existence, and work toward is yours for the taking and enjoying.*

BE PRACTICAL WHILE STARTING A BUSINESS

The purpose of the Law of Attraction teachings is to pump you up and get the right energy peaking, but even while working with the Law of Attraction for money manifestation, it is important to be practical. If you don't have a couple of years of extra cash stacked somewhere, don't give up your job and start a business unless you have someone to back you up financially. I have heard Law of Attraction coaches tell their stories of how they gave up their jobs and started earning six figure incomes, very quickly.

Maybe some can do that, but don't put yourself through that test. If you give up your job voluntarily, or sabotage it, and month one goes by, then month two, then months three, four and five and you don't have the kind of clientele you need, you will get into feeling stress and once stress sets in, you will end up attracting lack. So unless you have someone to pay your living costs, please stick to your daily job, the one that brings in the bread and butter, and puts a roof over your head, while working on your business simultaneously. Every situation is different and this is a general guideline to be applied appropriately.

You don't want to watch your bank balance go down, with very little, if any money coming in. Please don't depend only on your visualization skills to quickly manifest the kind of money you need to live on comfortably unless you are really good at it. I am not trying to frighten you here, but just asking you to be practical while using the Law of Attraction teachings to manifest a good life.

It is okay to combine magic and practicality. It is good to dream and think of magical possibilities, but you have to be careful before you embark on anything that takes you down the pathway to lack. It is a good idea to have money flowing in at all times. As you feel comfortable monetarily, you will be in a happy mood and able to think of money flowing in from your business (as you are not constantly watching your expenses be greater than your income). Make sure that you have adequate money at all times to cover your costs.

Like attracts like, and the presence of money attracts more money.

THE COMPANY YOU KEEP

The company you keep matters. If the money energy around you is empty, discover if you have any source of negative energy around you. Sometime's other people's poverty energy can affect you unless your energy is so strong as to overcome it. Don't try to be braver than you can be by taking on people who have a lot of poverty going on. It is good to help people, but try not to take on their negative money karma. Stay detached and don't get emotional (even while helping others) or you may start to attract their problems to you.

If your family is doing well monetarily, especially your parents, you can sometimes take shelter with them while you recover from money issues. If they can make you feel better by taking care of some of your basic expenses like food, shelter and medical, you will breathe more freely, reduce your fear, and attract abundance. It is not to make you dependent on them but to give you respite in order to get your money energy into balance again. If your soul mate (whether or not he is with you) does well monetarily, or has some good qualities that you can use, you can connect to him mentally and ask his energy to help you focus and make money.

ATTRACTING CLIENTS

Clients flow in a certain energy line. If you have different energies flowing around you, keeping you distracted, it may temporarily block your client energy. The best way to understand this is to think of lighting a jasmine incense stick. If you light a jasmine incense stick, there is no point lighting a lavender incense stick especially after the jasmine fragrance filled smoke is thick in your home because the lavender will find it hard to make itself known. Even if you have a somewhat equal mix of fragrances going on, it will be a mish-mash and not clear.

If you have different energies around you, the energy of your clients coming through may be difficult. Clear out the old energy and tune into the energy of your clients calling you. As you feel them around you, you will get contact. You can also think of money energy and gather it around you after clearing the air, and your clients will call as they could currently be the main source of your money.

To bring in your clients, feel their presence around you and keep your mind open to them. Many people want clients but don't want the work that goes with it. If you feel genuinely happy talking to your clients they will come to you. You can also think of how good it feels to enjoy hearing a particular client's voice; as you think of him, he will also think of you, and call you.

Be careful of the like and dislike energy you put out, because both have power. You can either attract clients that have good energy or clients that have negative energy. You can have clients that are rich and have money to spare to work with you, or clients that are always having a problem paying their bills. Tune into what you really want.

HAVING GOOD WORK KARMA HELPS

In order to do any job well, you must have the ability to do it. If your mind likes relaxing all the time and being lazy, you may not be able to get into abundant client energy, because to work with clients you have to maintain a high energy level and a mind that is alert and ready to solve any problem. This applies to any job that requires you to do a lot of work and to perform at high levels of mental and/or physical activity.

> *The best way to make money is to get up, shake your mind off dust, and work. This world needs to be maintained and you can select what you want to do to maintain it.*

Now your question to me will be- why should I read about money manifestation if I have to work anyway?

It is to be able to make ways for the money to come through. If you don't have good money karma, you will not be able to get the job that pays you well, or your business to run well. Yes there are casinos and lottery tickets that also bring in money, but you need to be aligned to winning money and not losing it, so be careful here. It's not about something being wrong or right but it's about being smart. Check to see if you are in the process of attracting something to you, or pushing it out. If you push things out, what you want keeps getting delayed more and more.

MAKING INTENTIONS

Once you have money flowing in at certain times, and with certain regularity, it's good to maintain that schedule. Energy can be trained or programmed to give you certain amounts of money at certain times but you must keep up that schedule, or retrain the energy to a new schedule to either increase the money coming in or alter the sources of the money coming in. It is always a good idea to keep one source constant bringing in the money while you play around with the other sources trying out different ideas.

> *Practice having control over your work energy instead of allowing chaos into it, because chaos energy creates confusion.*

You can make intentions about the amount of money you want to make in a certain year and over a period of time. As you make these intentions, your energy will get ready to attract it to you, getting you into the kind of business or work that you need to do to make that money.

If you feel restricted to live within a certain money ceiling, try this. Think of a lid placed over you preventing you from making more money, then lift your hands up straight and with some force hit upwards on that lid. You should feel better as you remove this false ceiling placed on you, limiting your income and keeping you stuck within certain levels. Do this as often as you need to. Also ensure that you are not subject to the belief systems of certain organizations that need you to believe in what they believe to fulfill their goals and objectives, however honorable. You need to have your own goals based on what you want to achieve in this life. Try not to be controlled by the minds of the leaders of these organizations and their followers. The leaders of such organizations are fulfilling their life purpose and not yours.

This holds true for every person and every situation that makes you believe that you can't do better in life and that you need to live in a certain way within certain limits. Get your mind together today because here is one truth-

There is nothing and nobody stopping you from making the kind of money that you have seen millionaires and billionaires make. Just be smart about it and look out for your ultimate good.

WATCH OUT FOR THE SNAKES AND THE CHUTES

Remember the game of life from chapter twelve? As you climb up using the ladders that you come across, certain negative energies may try to intervene and disrupt your work especially when you are getting ready to succeed.

This is not a sign from God to give up, so please don't give up. This is just the negative forces trying to make you think that you will not succeed. Sometimes there may be a lesson to learn from the negativity.

Remember that in truth nobody can really stop you from your dreams. Nobody can tell you that you cannot enjoy all that God has to offer. God is not poor, and he does not want you to have a poverty mindset. God's vault is open to you for you to enjoy. Get up, dust off your pants and continue walking towards your goal.

You are meant to have all that an abundant mindset can enjoy. Just create that mindset and don't give up. Money is not bad, it is good. It will help you provide the kind of life that you want for yourself and your family. Tap into the money line now and give up all the poverty oaths taken in past lives and in this one.

An affirmation:

"I allow myself to become rich now. I allow all the goodness of money and its equivalents to enter my life now. I am rich and happy now."

PART IV

The Land of Joy
and Miracles

"I'm here to stay!"

Chapter Twenty–Nine

~

How it Feels Here

"I am in the land of joy. It feels good to be here."

Joyful Manifestation happens when you reach the vibration of joy and fuel your life with that joy. When you think of a life area, if you can feel joy and confidence, it means that you are in the space of Joyful Manifestation, and your attraction factor for that life area is positive.

How does it feel to be in the land of joy?

Being in the land of joy feels like you have God living with you all the time, in your heart, infusing your body and mind with bubbles of happiness. Everything feels good, and you feel confident that things go well for you because you matter to the universe. It feels as if you are the most important person in this world and if you were not there, this world would not exist. It feels as if everything happens only for you, for your survival and happiness, as if the whole universe re-arranges itself again and again, just for your joy. It is **your light** which, being so strong and steady, lights up everything around you, for you to witness and enjoy and for your loved ones to bask in. Your mind feels good to you (you love living in it), and all the cells in your body rejoice because of the sheer joy of being alive. Joyful events happen all by themselves because that is how you intended it.

With the ten step Joyful Manifestation process, you can access this land of joy anytime. You can work on each life area and bring them into the space of joy even if you did not feel confident about them before. For example, while writing this book I went through many stages. There were times when I just did not feel like writing because life was happening to me. As I resolved each life area and felt good about life itself, I could put in the work required to complete the book without worrying about how the book would come out into the market. Somehow I knew that as I reached the completion of this book, forces would gather together to get my book out. I knew it with a certainty and I expected it to happen, because *hello!* Magic happens all the time!

This world is magical, and as you allow yourself to believe that this world is magical, you will start to see magic happen all around you. There is a God, and he's right here with you, with us all. In fact, he is the All. He is everywhere and is everyone. He is in you and in all of his creations, and he cares. He really cares for us—for you.

I ask that you just believe this truth that God cares.

He has sent and continues to send writers, teachers, coaches, and healers to help people who feel sad and despondent, and as if nothing good happens. There is no limit to the teachings that God makes available to you. Truth is one, and the basic teachings are one, but they are altered a little bit according to the times and needs of people. People have asked for help for years, and so he sent help in the form of information and ideas. Creation is infused with knowledge, and he makes it available in many ways.

You ask for love and it is given. You ask for guidance and it is given. You ask for help and it is given. You ask for your Self and it is given. Anytime you feel love and joy in your heart, know that it is God responding and communicating. He speaks to you, the physical self, through your feelings and that is why you can feel an opening in the heart and a joyful, light feeling when you release resistances. This is a great place to be to spin wonderful dreams, and could mean that what you have asked for has been sanctioned and is coming in. Just know that when it is sanctioned (by your Self) it is in energy form soon to be manifested into physical form, and sometimes the happening is so fast that you don't realize it. Just be physically and mentally ready to receive what you asked for. If you need training or need to learn certain skills to handle what you asked for, get those skills into place, because your gift will arrive any moment and when it does, the universe does not want you to be unprepared.

Joy creates joyful situations. Use the Joyful Manifestation process to manifest what you want.

Chapter Thirty

~

Maintaining Your Joy

"Now that I am here in the land of joy, I put my flag in and make this my home. I maintain my home well."

Once you feel joy, it becomes addictive and you will not settle for less. Yes, there may be times when you are not completely anchored in your joy, but you will not allow such states of un-joy for very long. Once you have tasted joy, you will put in every effort to climb back up the ladder again; there is no other way that you will have it because feeling peace, happiness and glorious joy soon becomes your way of life.

Now that you know the steps to Joyful Manifestation, you can start applying its principles without getting into such a bad state that you are forced to let go of people and things permanently. You will be alert to the conditions of your manifestations and can use the Joyful Manifestation process before you reach a stage of really heavy negativity with regard to any life area. You know that when certain life areas are not working well you can get them back into working order.

Enjoy your amazing nervous system and body. Take care of it knowing that God lives within you. Treat your body like a Divine temple and bow down to yourself and all of creation.

All of creation is alive. Never be fooled into thinking otherwise.

You don't have to master everything in life, just the capacity to remain happy and be persistent in a good way. If you feel that you are on a spinning wheel having to constantly master and overcome situations, then let go of that vibration also, as it too can become an energy that you can get stuck in. Realize when you are spending all your time just mastering situations and come out of that need.

Enjoy your Divine Self now. Visualize golden rays of your Divine Self spreading out and permeating every living creature with its love, and just know that every living creature loves you. There is no dearth of love, because love abounds everywhere. You are love, and you are joy.

Continue enjoying your joy!

Chapter Thirty-One

Expansion and Success in Material Life

"I stay in the land of joy and bring this joy into all my activities."

There are many schools of thought about material success and whether it goes against spirituality. While there may always be different ways of thinking about this subject, here is one formula that you can apply.

Spiritual success helps create and maintain physical success.

Everything is spirit, and in this spirit filled world, if you want anything to move and become something that you want, you have to work with spirit. Spirit moves people, places, and things. Spirit forms into people, places, and things.

Yes, there are several successful people who are atheists and don't believe in God/Spirit, but even they are using certain basic laws of spiritual success.

With or without being conscious of using spirit, they are doing it all the time. They are using their mind (which is spirit) to direct thoughts (which is spirit) to gain material success (which is again spirit vibrating as dense material form). Everywhere they go they are encountering spirit, because there is no place that spirit is not.

The reason that it pays to work with spirit consciously is that there is less trial and error, and more consistent success.

Further, many who don't connect to spirit consciously are still searching for their joy. Yes, I know that they will say, "I am happy" but unless people experience the ecstatic states of divine love and joy, they are not in touch with their True Self. They stumble along life constantly coping, becoming happy and sad with each event, not anchored in their joy.

> *You can look into a person's eyes and see if they are truly experiencing their joyful nature and divine love.*

When you start the journey toward joy, you will experience it again and again, feeling it in your heart. It will also be reflected in your face and people looking at you will know that you are anchored in your joy.

> *Just start the journey; everything else will fall into place.*

The soul always wants to expand because that's its nature. That's God's nature. So living a limited life does not serve anybody, neither you nor anyone else. Material success is good because it serves everyone to be in abundance.

Here are some success tips that you can use:

1. Drop the false humility. You are serving no one.

2. Be confident, but not arrogant. Arrogance is just a cover up for insecurity.

3. Develop your sense of confidence from knowing who you really are, and with that in mind, build on your physical success also.

4. See everything that you have and are creating as a projection of that Divine energy and feel good about it.

5. Feel good about everything, and when you encounter darkness, ask that it reveal its lesson and turn into light.

6. Remove all false boundaries that exist in your mind. These are ceilings placed by the conditions of your birth, your age, your past, the society, and other seeming failures in your life. Just because you have never made 'big' money, does not mean that you cannot do it now. Remove all mental ceilings that hold you back from your success.

7. Whatever work you do, know that you are contributing to the betterment of this world. God wants this world to work well and that is why there are so many people contributing to this world and its working.

8. You can have open talks with God and even sulk if you like, but always come back to the space of joy, because you are at your most powerful in this space.

9. Positive ego is good; negative ego will work against you.

10. Open your doors to receiving good. There is no harm in being wealthy, because God is all about abundance. Just imagine if you were God, you would be scratching your head wondering why your creations are so poor when you have provided so much.

11. Poverty comes from a poor mindset. Change your mind.

12. There is plenty for everyone. There is no need to get into unnecessary push and pull situations creating negative energy. If something is yours, it will come to you. Just float good energy toward it or toward that life area in general.

13. There is abundance everywhere. Get used to this truth.

14. Don't worry if someone hurts you. Each person reaps the karma arising from his personality, and will get only what is due to him. Release him from your experience and continue toward your joy.

15. Keep developing the skills required for you to do your work well.

16. Don't feel pressured to always 'conform'. Adherence to law is good, and is different from being pressured to live in the box.

17. There is no need to get stressed over things that are not working well. If you see something that you don't like, float a new intention about what you'd like to see happen, and watch the Divine forces take over and do the job for you.

18. Remember that consciousness is ever-changing and shifting, and know that today's evils may not be there tomorrow. For example, while the police still need to catch criminals, this may not be needed as much a few years from now, as people may become more aware of the need to maintain peace and order without being forced to do so.

19. Be okay with today without being disturbed about tomorrow. Your dreams will come true. Give it a chance.

20. Use every small success to build up more success. Learn from your failures, but don't carry them with you as your cross. Put down your cross.

21. There is no need to keep connecting to people who don't represent true joy. Connect to those you know are joyful. The days for sacrifice from the space of suffering are over. Connect to happy and loving energies so that you have enough happiness to share.

22. Shout "Woo hoo!" whenever you see someone else succeed. This way you connect to their success instead of feeling bad about it. And remember that it could be you succeeding tomorrow, and you would love to hear people cheer for you.

23. Discover your source of Divine love and keep connecting to it. You are love. You are joy.

24. It is okay to charge fees for the services that you provide to this world. Understand that if you carry any energy in you which says, "It is okay to not receive proper remuneration for work that I do", that is what you may attract (unless that is what you really want). The energy of martyrdom is carried by many, and is unnecessary.

25. Be a Master Manifester and not a Master Unmanifester. Understand and recognize when you are in the process of manifesting and when you are in the process of unmanifesting.

26. See everything as a gift from the Divine as it makes it easy for you to do your work. If you carry the burden of every single action, it may become difficult for you. Learn to balance personal responsibility with the universe's responsibility, and you will succeed in life with an ease that even the most successful will want to emulate.

Chapter Thirty-Two

~

Taking it to the World

"I am a source of joy to everyone
and everything."

Whatever you learn, whatever you know, if you share it with the world, it will come back to you many times over. Think of all the diseases and problems that are easily solved compared to a few years ago when there were no solutions. These solutions exist because people have spent time thinking, intending, working, and contributing to this world. Contemplating this is humbling, yet a matter for rejoicing that some people cared so much for you and your loved ones that they spent a lot of time and effort researching. Yes it's true that many are compensated for their efforts with money and fame, but they did spend many years thinking of solutions before they came into their good fortune.

Don't hoard what you have learned. Give freely of it to the world and watch it take root in the minds of people, filling their lives with light and happiness.

Just keep asking: "How may I serve?"

When you bring information to the world, don't force it on people. There is no need to create a new religion, and there is no need to force your religion down anyone's throat either. Just help them access their inner joy. Giving people health tips, healing energy, knowledge, etc., is good, but not with the threat of going to hell if they don't follow your words.

Hell exists only in people's minds, which then affects their lives. Just help free them from the issues in their minds and show them the joy that exists within them ready to be accessed anytime. The rewards are plenty as the Divine gives you unlimited joy in return.

You are feeling the Divine when you experience joy. The Divine is always there; he just wants you to know it, and he does this by allowing you to feel your joy from him, the Source of it all. Just remain as connected to him as you possibly can and you will be okay.

> *He is Source. He is joy. He is nothing. He is everything. He is in everything. He is in you. He is you. You are him. He is the All.*

BEING JOY AND CELEBRATING

Joy is the key for successful manifestation; sadness is not a good attractor of joyful events, so be in joy and celebrate. Sing, laugh, dance and make happiness your way of life but with a good dose of keeping your eyes on your goals. There are people who are happy but this happiness comes from not taking on any task at all. It's easy to be happy when you do nothing but that's not the kind of happiness we are talking about here, we are talking about being happy and materially successful at the same time.

Some Keys to Joyful Manifestation

1. Switch to joy in the midst of dealing with what you don't like. This will bring in what you ask for.

2. Connect to Source and gain its wisdom even if your mind is in turmoil. At the very least, even if you can't access your joy, work on calming your mind because the turmoil is not the truth.

3. Come back to your center quickly after an unpleasant event.

4. Bring understanding to a situation and discover what you will like to see happen.

5. Know that the situation is just a projection of consciousness, and as consciousness changes, so will the situation.

6. Reach for better thoughts and move toward the feeling of relief. Don't get stuck in negative feelings.

7. See the Divine in all situations, and even if you do forget Source for a while, reconnect yourself quickly as soon as you remember to do so.

8. See the teachings behind situations and incorporate them into your life. Any change in consciousness means a change in your reality.

9. See this world as belonging to the Divine, and yourself as playing your part in it.

Your nervous system is designed to experience joy in all glory. You are here to experience joy but even while you experience joy in the people and things in your life, don't be fooled that they are the sole cause of your joy. They are not the main cause of your joy they are just beautiful mirrors that reflect your joy back to you. Knowing this, don't get attached to people or things to your detriment. Instead, radiate the feeling that you love to experience joy through this person, and the Divine will listen. The Divine loves you.

He wants you to be happy because you contribute greatly to the happiness in this world.

Everything is consciousness and consciousness loves to celebrate—itself. You are joy!

There is nobody more beautiful than you, dear one. There is nobody more loved, so celebrate yourself—now!